CARPE WEEKEND

52 DAY TRIPS AND ADVENTURES NEAR WASHINGTON, DC

Elaine C. Jean

Photography by Paul N. Jean

D1057392

ISBN-10: 1484003969

ISBN-13: 978-1484003961

DEDICATION

For Paul Jean: You're my soul mate, photographer and travel companion on the great journey of life.

CARPE WEEKEND
52 DAY TRIPS AND ADVENTURES
NEAR WASHINGTON, DC

A Roamingtheplanet.com Guide

Table of Contents

ACKNOWLEDGMENTS

Good friends give us energy and inspiration. They contribute to who we are and what we believe we can accomplish. They enhance the good times and soften the bad. The best of friends take time out from their busy schedules to encourage our endeavors, helping us to see the value of humor and of a life well lived. I am fortunate to have a strong circle of friends in my life; among them are Terri, Jim and Niki Galvin, Mary Lynn Janovec, Pam and Mark Jenkins, Carol and Dave Kee and Jana and Ed Rezac.

Lucky is the person who has a loving and supportive family; even luckier is the person who has a loving and supportive family with solid skills. Thank you to my daughter, Nikki Jean, for her artistic eye and whimsical logo, and to my son, David Jean, for his formidable IT skills. Their enthusiasm for and support of this project are much appreciated.

Thanks to my husband, Paul Jean, for his clear, crisp and insightful photography, his fearless urban driving techniques, his talent for design and layout, his dogged determination and his eternal optimism. Without him, this book simply would not exist.

It would also not exist without the encouragement of my good friend and *Loudoun Times-Mirror* Editor John Geddie, who assigned my first local travel story for the *Loudoun Independent* in 2010. Also, thanks to Editor Steve Cahill for my column in the *Fairfax County Times*. His deadlines and kind words kept me upbeat and on track.

All good books have an eagle-eye team of initial reviewers to proofread and comment. Thank you to Nikki Jean, Jim Kurtz and Theda Parish for serving as my nit-picky focus group.

Finally, thank you to the thousands of people I've met during more than 80 day trips spanning a period of two years. Museum curators, assembly line workers and aerial acrobats – as well as the makers of craft beer, moonshine and fine wine – opened their worlds to me. And it was often the fleeting interaction with other sightseers that made the visits particularly memorable. Thank you to all for generously sharing your time, your stories and your passions!

INTRODUCTION

Carpe Weekend is an antidote to the wanderlust that haunts me, that edgy feeling of a weekend fast approaching with no particular place to go. For more than two years, Paul and I have taken full advantage of the 60-hour block of personal time between clocking out on Friday evening and rising to the alarm on Monday morning. We've claimed it as our own.

I've planned each trip – the majority are one-day excursions, but a few are weekend-long adventures – to carry a consistent theme and tone. Most are happy romps, while some are thought-provoking journeys that offer a sampling of different times, places and lives. All are intended to entertain, educate and open the door to further exploration.

Paul's photography is more than a supplement to my writing; it's an enhancement that offers his unique perspective on our journeys. A look through his lens inspires the reader to cast aside responsibilities and take to the road.

This book is not a travel guide, rather a personal account of our travel experiences. It should not be seen as a replacement for *Fodor's* and *Frommer's*, although either would make an excellent companion piece to *Carpe Weekend* for their broad coverage of popular travel destinations. And, of course, it's always a good idea to check individual websites for current information regarding hours of operation, admission fees and changes in policies before setting out on any adventure.

Put simply, *Carpe Weekend* is a series of essays that's intended as a catalyst. For us, it has become a way of life. In the process of tripping, we've chatted with many of the interesting people we've met along the way – a woman in Winchester, Virginia, who swore she had the real scoop on local legend Patsy Cline, and the three guys in a nearby town who were dodging their wives while hiding out in the back room of a tobacco shop, to name just a few. The field work has been our great pleasure.

From the time we are young, we're taught not to talk to strangers – sound advice for children. Unfortunately, it can become a habit that's hard to break. In this fast-paced, ever-changing Facebook-y world in which we live, I enjoy forging real connections with the people and places around me. These unexpected interactions serve to brighten my days and enhance my life, illustrating that we're all a lot more alike than we are different.

Most importantly, I've found that when I talk to strangers, they often become my friends!

Elaine

This marketing oddity at Leesburg Cigar and Pipe sets the tone for the day.

1. PROOF WE ARE ALIVE

The Badass Tour: Hand-rolled cigars, hooch and horses

Most New Year's resolutions go by the wayside, and old habits return with a vengeance. Why not skip the outdated ritual this year and start a new one? Embrace your inner badass with a tour of some of the finest vices the Mid-Atlantic region has to offer.

Abraham Lincoln once observed that, "Folks who have no vices have very few virtues." So in the interest of improving my character, I headed out to historic Leesburg, Virginia and wild and wonderful West Virginia with some of my favorite friends.

Whether you're a newbie or a chimney, the knowledgeable staff at **Leesburg Cigar and Pipe** (205 Harrison Street SE) matches customers up with the perfect smoke. This boutique tobacconist offers a huge selection of cigars and cigarillos, as well as pipes, tobacco, imported cigarettes and accessories. The walk-in humidor is one of the largest in the area, keeping cigars fresh and well hydrated.

The shop is comfortably situated in an old station master's house and appointed with rich leather seating and a big screen plasma TV. Manly? Yes. But I like it, too …

Everything about the **Bloomery Plantation Distillery** in Charles Town, West Virginia (16357 Charles Town Road) is unexpected, from the diminutive 1840s log cabin to the handcrafted fruit cordials it produces. And if the word cordial conjures memories of grandma's after dinner drinks, think again. Unless your grandmother is a nana and she hails from the old country.

The Bloomery Plantation Distillery sells handcrafted cellos from their restored log cabin near the Shenandoah River.

When Linda Losey and Tom Kiefer traveled to Italy for the canonization of his great-great aunt – now Saint Mary of the Cross – they returned with a thirst for limoncello that the local stores just couldn't quench. In fact, they didn't find a single drop that lived up to its Italian counterpart. So they made their own. And it was very good.

Linda's next step was to buy a ramshackle log cabin and 12 acres of land via Craig's list. Then she hired Rob Losey, her ex-husband, to cultivate 2,000 Caroline raspberry plants. She proceeded to buy a greenhouse, haul it back to the farm, fill said greenhouse with 40 Santa Theresa lemon trees and hang a shingle out by the road.

Of course. Because that's what I do when I'm craving a drink.

No matter how crazy it all sounds, it was absolutely brilliant. And so are the flavors you'll sample while gathered around a cozy woodstove in the restored cabin's tasting room. Linda crafts her cellos to capture the essence of each flavor in a way that's pure, clear and bright – but never bitter – using organic fruit, zesting lemons by hand and avoiding the nasty pith.

She gives tours of the grounds, pointing out that the original structure is one of only two slave quarters remaining in Jefferson County, with siding salvaged from an old C&O canal boat to expand the living quarters. Linda welcomes you into her greenhouse, where she lovingly tends trees that yield some of the produce for her heavenly hooch.

Rob mans the bar – doling out samples of the fruits of their labor, sharing recipes and exercising a quick wit alongside Rita, his significant other. Tom's often there, too, and the group looks like one big happy family. Their motto might as well be carved over the bar: All you need is cello.

Rita and Linda pour samples as Rob waxes poetic about Linda's talent for making limoncello.

Free tours and tastings are offered on Fridays and Saturdays, with a line-up of SweetShines that include the Limoncello that started it all, as well as Ginger Shine, Cremma Lemma (aka Moonshine Milkshake), Hard Lemonade and Chocolate Raspberry Cello. All are available to purchase by the bottle for consumption at home. Live music – folk rock, reggae, blues and soul – is enjoyed with coffee in the evening.

You may want to bring a sense of humor to the Bloomery. These folks own a couple of spiffy lemon costumes, and they're not afraid to use them. You might just end up wearing one before the visit is over.

Entering **Hollywood Casino at Charles Town Races** (750 Hollywood Drive) is, for the uninitiated, a bit like falling down the rabbit hole. Plastic palm trees and counterfeit cacti fringe rows of one armed bandits – over 3,500 video slot machines in all – with names like *Vegas Shindig, Super Fireball Frenzy* and *Unicorn Dreaming*.

My tip: Stay away from themes that ooze cuteness; I lost a fair share of money on *Dog Days* just trying to see the Goldendoodle prance when I scored three in a row. Gambling is an emotional sport and, in retrospect, I may have been better off with the homage to John Wayne. But I can't prove it. Win, lose or draw, you'll be entertained by the new and improved venue.

In 1997 Penn National Gaming bet on a comeback for Charles Town Races, purchasing the facility and beginning a $175-million upgrade. In 2010 table games – including poker, blackjack, mini-baccarat and roulette – made their debut, and today the venue features simulcast racing, numerous dining options and two huge parking garages. The three-quarter-mile race track draws some of the finest trainers, horses and jockeys on the East Coast.

Book a table in the Skyline Terrace for dinner with an expansive view of the race track. The restaurant offers a full menu from Tuesday through Saturday and, on Friday and Saturday nights, a prime rib and seafood buffet that reaches from here to there and back again.

Bets may be placed with tellers next to the Poker Room on the same level, but for the ultimate experience call ahead and reserve a big table with its own betting machine. Upon arrival, set up an account and load a debit card with the evening's mad money for one-swipe gambling.

The dining room is designated nonsmoking, but you can light up down on the apron of the track – where the action is. You may even pick up a few tips on upcoming races from the regulars.

Hand-rolled cigars, hooch and horse racing – it's the perfect trifecta of vices. Whether you're truly a badass or merely a wannabe, I'm willing to wager this is a day trip you'll remember – and want to repeat – as a chaser to thrown-over New Year's resolutions or an alternative to those that would have been doomed from the start.

FYI:

- This trip is best made on a Friday or Saturday afternoon.
- Leesburg Cigar and Pipe is in Market Station and is open daily.
- Hollywood Casino is open 24/7; anyone under 21 will not be admitted.
- Skyline Terrace is closed on Sundays and Mondays.
- Several other restaurants are on site, as well as a food court.
- Live races are held year round, and post time varies with the season.
- Visit www.hollywoodcasinocharlestown.com to see race schedules and to make dinner reservations for Skyline Terrace.

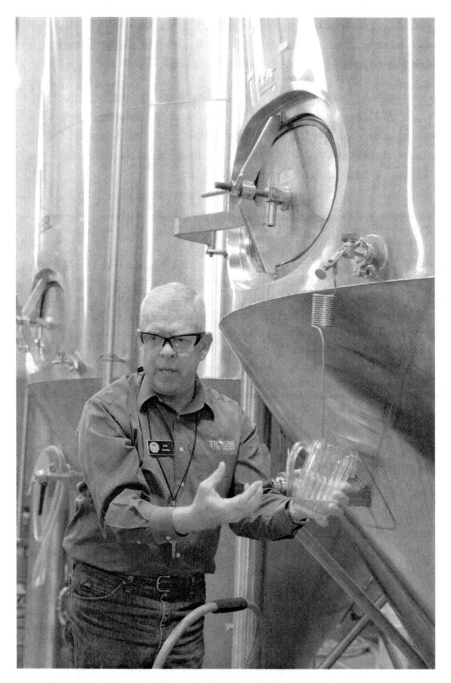

Our Troegs' tour guide, Quarter Keg Bob, collects a sample of ale for tasting.

Lancaster County: Hopping through Pennsylvania

Harrisburg boasts more microbreweries than the average burg, with pubs large and small dotting the hills and valleys of its surrounding countryside. This is an educational day trip that scratches the tip of a foamy iceberg and proves that learning can be fun.

The rich brewing tradition of Pennsylvania's capital city dates back to the 18th century. In 1705 John Harris established his trading post here, and you gotta wonder if he had a little somethin'-somethin' on tap. By the middle of the 19th century Lancaster County had been dubbed the Munich of America, with beers winning acclaim both in the United States and abroad.

Support of the World War I effort took a significant toll on the country's brewing industry, and Prohibition put another nail in the coffin in 1920. Graupner's was Harrisburg's last brewery standing when it shut its doors in 1951, making this one thirsty town until the microbrewery craze of the 1990s hit.

Today industrious residents have put their old factory space to good use, producing an impressive array of handcrafted beers. Take a Saturday road trip and taste them for yourself, commandeering a minivan and filling it with friends to make the experience even more memorable.

This is the proper use of the ubiquitous suburban peoplemover – comfortable seating for six of your best beer-loving buddies. Choose passengers wisely, as the journey provides half the fun – and potentially all the psychological trauma.

Harrisburg is located on the east bank of the Susquehanna River, an easy drive from almost anywhere. Our recommended day trip begins here and includes several fine breweries with deep ties to the region.

The **Appalachian Brewing Company** (50 N. Cameron Street) is housed in a three-story antique brick-and-timber building that was formerly home to the Auchenbach Printing Company. Destroyed by fire in the 1930s and rebuilt for use by the Works Project Administration, it has also turned out parts for WWII aircraft. Fire again ripped through the building in 1993, rendering it nearly useless.

The taps at Appalachian Brewing Company deliver everything from Birch Beer to Susquehanna Stout in style.

The process of restoration and renewal began in 1995 when four partners purchased the building for $1 and put their blood, sweat, tears – and $1 million – into a project that subsequently earned the Mayor's Award for Preservation Excellence. Appalachian Brewing Company's first batch of beer was released in 1997, and the rest is history. ABC is now one of the largest microbreweries in the nation, producing flagship and specialty beers and craft sodas from its facility.

ABC's Harrisburg location offers free tours every Saturday at 1 p.m., providing a step-by-step look at how great beverages are made. Soda tastings are given at the end of the tour, with beer for those with proper ID. Be sure to arrive at least 10 minutes early, as space is limited.

The brewpub is a thing of beauty, with exposed brick walls throughout, massive wooden beams overhead and aged hardwood floors under foot. With historic property and a checkered past often come paranormal activity, and ABC is rumored to have a ghost of its own.

While history and beery goodness envelop you, this brewery is serious about its food, too. Offerings include appetizers – the Thai chicken wings rock—as well as soups, salads, sandwiches, burgers, pizza and other comfort foods to compliment pints and flights. The beer sampler includes seven tastes of the flagship brews, including Susquehanna Stout (affectionately referred to as hair of the dog), Organic Brown Ale and Hoppy Trails IPA. The root beer is both a palate cleanser and a bonus.

Brothers John and Chris Trogner founded **Troegs Brewing Company** in Harrisburg, but they've since moved to a state-of-the-art facility in the former commissary in Hershey (200 E. Hershey Park Drive). Like ABC, their first batch was released in 1997 – a very good year for beer lovers.

You can watch the Troegs Brewing Company's bottling line operate as part of the tour, whether you have a guide or not.

The tasting room is packed with people and activity, and you know from the moment you walk in that this is a happening place. Because Troegs is so popular, reservations for a guided tour are recommended and may be made online. Tickets are picked up and paid for in the gift shop on the day of your visit.

A tour of the impressive new facility is nothing short of awe inspiring. A knowledgeable guide leads the way and confirms a philosophy that the brothers have shared since the beginning: If we don't like it, we don't make it. With their taste buds as compass and themselves as critic, John and Chris continue to create a balanced selection of innovative beers that pleases most everyone.

Two scientists in a sparkling microbiology lab are the cornerstone of the operation, ensuring quality by analyzing beer during the fermentation process and as a finished product. With a Troegs beer, you never have to wonder if the brew lives up to the label.

Popular favorites include Hopback Amber, Javahead Stout and that holiday darling, Mad Elf. The Scratch series is an experimental line that's not sold in stores and allows the brewers the opportunity to play with interesting flavors and techniques.

A trip across the brew deck reveals a look at the process from mash tun to lauter tun to brew kettle, and home brewers will probably become giddy with excitement. Of particular interest is a sexy hop doser that adds the bite to beer, and if you're lucky you'll get to see it in action.

Their high-tech approach means that Troegs brews a consistently good product, but they still test it the old-fashioned way – they taste it. Because, at the end of the day, it's all about the flavor.

The guided tour is highly recommended, and a souvenir glass and beer tasting is included. Note that you'll also get to try three levels of malted barley and sniff a jar of hops, but whatever you do, do not eat the hops. Trust me on this.

If you don't have the opportunity to book a tour ahead of time, the self-guided tour with interpretive signage does a pretty good job. And all roads lead to a great pub. The light menu features soups, salads, sandwiches and tasty snacks such as Mad Elf Fondue and Troegswurst.

About 20 minutes from Troegs in the small town of Mount Joy, **Bube's Brewery** (102 N. Market Street) – it's pronounced exactly the way you hope it's not – is worthy of exploration. Listed on the National Register of Historic Places, the nearly 150-year-old building is as much a museum as it is a restaurant and brewpub. Before you settle in to eat and drink, visit the gallery of artwork and walk among huge wooden vats that were once used to age beer. This is the only lager-era brewery left in America, and it's remarkably intact.

These large wooden vats were used to store German-style lager beer until the original Bube's Brewery closed in 1920, just before Prohibition.

The Catacombs Restaurant is actually a stone-lined vault that's 43 feet below street level, ideal for the cold storage that founder Alois Bube required for his beers. Open every evening for fine dining and offering themed dinners on occasion, the emphasis here is on good food and fun. Past events have included medieval feasts, with special celebrations on Halloween and during the Christmas season. Murder mystery dinners are held in the Alois Martini Bar.

Or opt for one of Bube's brews upstairs in the historic Bottling Works, along with a more casual menu that includes wings, pizza, poppers and frickles to share with friends, as well as soups, salads, sandwiches and entrees. The adjacent outdoor Biergarten is reminiscent of a Bavarian watering hole and showcases the original boiler and smokestack used to power the old brewery.

Bube's Brewery has been featured on the popular TV series *Ghosthunters*, and the investigative team revealed that Alois Bube may still be watching over his legacy. Jean Ellis – the great-granddaughter of the founder – leads ghost tours at Bube's every month and has collected tales of hauntings and published them in a book, *Spirits in Brewery*, available for $6.

Bube's Brewery provides a comfortable stop for happy wanderers, and the owner may even put you up for the night on the third floor with some advance notice. Probably a good idea, after a day of sampling Pennsylvania's finest.

While each person on our adventure had a favorite brew and brewery, we came to the conclusion that there really is no bad beer in Amish country. The region offers a great selection of handcrafted brews in a wide range of historic and high-tech backdrops that add to the ambiance.

So jump in the van and designate a driver. Even if you aren't a beer geek, you'll enjoy a great day with good friends. And don't forget to pack the growlers – reasonably priced refills are available at most locations.

The Lancaster Brewing Company, housed in an old tobacco barn in Lancaster, is a comfortable setting for dinner.

FYI:

- Make this trip on a Saturday to enjoy all its elements.
- ABC has more than one brewpub in Lancaster County.
- Reservations for ABC tours are made on the same day, so arrive early.
- Reserve tours of Troegs online; choose an early time to avoid crowds.
- Wander around Bube's Brewery on your own or ask for a guided tour.
- Tour fees vary by brewery, and flights are available for a small charge.
- Visit www.abcbrew.com, www.troegs.com and
  www.bubesbrewery.com for additional information.

Carpe Weekend's tip:

While **Lancaster Brewing Company** has a presence in Harrisburg, it's a small outpost and lacks the setting required for a proper brewery hop. If you have the time, drive to their Lancaster location (302 N. Plum Street). Warmth emanates from the former 19th century tobacco barn. Tours are available upon request, and a sampler includes some creative offerings. Milk Stout and Strawberry Wheat are in the line-up, and when mixed together they yield something akin to a beery strawberry milkshake. Visit www.lancasterbrewing.com for details.

Chuck Miller is the star of his own tour, leading guests through the process of making moonshine and whiskey.

Stillhouse at Belmont Farm: A whiff of the past

On this day trip you'll experience honest-to-goodness small town America in Fauquier County, and then visit a Culpeper farm where the owner turns out moonshine just like his Grampy used to make. Today is the day to, "Meet Virginia!"

Remington is a time capsule of a town – made obsolete by the new highway like so many of the good ones are. Found a half-mile down Freemans Ford Road off Route 29, a block of turn-of-the-century buildings gives a glimpse of a thriving past and reveals traces of Remington's role as a transportation hub.

Stop by the **Farmer's Wife** (204 E. Main Street) – open weekdays and Saturdays – and browse the aisles of this vintage grocery store. Lori Andes has assembled an impressive array of local, organic, natural and gluten-free items and baked goods in the store that her step-grandmother once owned.

Grab coffee and a fresh apple turnover and stay for a bit at one of the tables in the window, where you'll look out on a town that appears much the same as it did decades ago. After breakfast walk around and explore Remington Drug, with its nostalgia-inducing soda fountain, and Groves Hardware, with its time-worn wooden floors. The barber shop and a variety store will make you feel like you've been transported to Mayberry RFD.

About 12 miles east and hidden on a scenic country road on the outskirts of Culpeper, Chuck Miller pays homage to his grandfather's legacy and the Commonwealth of Virginia's heritage by making moonshine with his own twist – an ABC license.

At the Farmer's Wife in both Remington and Culpeper, Lori Andes still does business the old fashioned way.

Stillhouse Distillery at Belmont Farm (13490 Cedar Run Road) produces its moonshine in an authentic 2,000-gallon copper still – circa 1933 – using the same recipe Miller's grandfather did during Prohibition. The result is a product that will probably put hair on your chest. And if you didn't want hair on your chest, that's just too bad.

The newest offering, Stillhouse Original Moonshine, is "distilled four times to reach perfection." I bought a bottle and did, indeed, find the premium moonshine to be a more perfect way to put hair on your chest.

Moonshine is made from corn, and this corn is raised, grown, ground and fermented on Miller's 124-acre family farm. Lively tours by the Moonshine Man himself appeal to everyone from hardcore history buffs to weekend motorcycle groups.

Every hour on the hour Miller dances through his distillery, dishing out anecdotes sprinkled with family secrets. This is clearly a man who loves what he does, and he may just be the highlight of the day.

The free tour lends insight on Virginia's past, since the making and moving of moonshine is inextricably tied to the flavor of the Old Dominion state. Runners supercharged their cars to evade local law enforcement during the era of Prohibition, and when the need to speed was no longer a job requirement the great sport of NASCAR racing was born.

The quaintness of Belmont Farm, combined with the folksy friendliness of its host and his wife, make their booze seem downright wholesome. Paradoxically, the unmistakably sweet-sour smell of mash and the woodsy aroma of aging whiskey are nearly intoxicating.

Bottling takes place every Wednesday on antique equipment and is described by the owner as a rather intense workout. You may watch the process through a small window but will not be allowed in the bottling room, for your own safety.

A picturesque horse barn hints at life on the Miller family farm.

A gift shop sells the usual souvenirs along with a few more spirited ones, and features a display of arrowheads and Civil War artifacts. A small photo gallery gives its owner bragging rights, with pictures that include at least one president and an author famous for her forensic mysteries.

You can buy White Lightning and Kopper Kettle – as well as Stillhouse Original Moonshine – for sipping on your own front porch. Belmont Farm is open daily, Tuesday through Saturday, and closed on Sundays and Mondays.

Downtown Culpeper is a day-trip-within-a-day-trip. Pick up a map at the train depot and explore the many and varied antique stores, gourmet shops and purveyors of pottery, clothing and international arts and crafts. And when it comes time to eat, Culpeper's got you covered.

The Hazel River Inn (195 E. Davis Street) is located in the oldest commercial building in town and occupies a lot that was once surveyed by a young George Washington. In 1790 an addition was tacked on for use as a tobacco warehouse.

The Hazel River Inn will put you in touch with Historic Culpeper, and with some of the spirits who dwell there.

The basement served as a jail for both the Union and the Confederacy during the Civil War, and it's now home to a ghost or two, along with a pub serving casual food, microbrews and live music on Friday and Saturday nights. Lunch is offered starting at noon on the weekends.

The dining room, a hardware store for many years, is warm and welcoming with exposed brick walls, a centrally located fireplace and an upscale menu. It's open Thursday through Sunday for lunch and dinner.

Before heading home, linger a bit in the town. New stores open on a regular basis, so it's worth exploring even if you've been to Culpeper before.

FYI:

- This trip is best made Thursday – Saturday from April – December.
- The Farmer's Wife in Remington is closed on Sundays.
- Their Culpeper outpost, at 105 E. Davis Street, is closed on Mondays.
- The Hazel River Inn is closed on Tuesdays and Wednesdays.
- Stillhouse is open Tuesday – Saturday, from April – December.
- Reservations aren't required, but there's no harm in calling.
- Visit www.moonshine.com for information about the history of moonshine and recipes for enjoying it.

Jim Corcoran, CTO and all-around great guy, mixes business with pleasure for serious fun at Corcoran Brewing Company.

LoCo, Virginia: A beery good trip to wine country

Explore the countryside of Northern Virginia and discover the unexpected – a patch of hops among the vineyards, bodacious BBQ in farm country and vintage hip five miles north of mega-mall madness.

Loudoun County is home to over 25 wineries, producing some mighty fine fruit of the vine. Judging by the number of grape vines in the Commonwealth, you'd think we're in a vinocentric state of mind. But Jim Corcoran's out to change that.

Corcoran takes his role as CTO – Chief Tasting Officer – of the **Corcoran Brewing Company** (14635 Corkys Farm Lane) seriously – at times drinking as much as a keg of beer a week. It's all in the interest of research and development, of course …

Dozens of breweries are dedicated to the art of handcrafting microbrews, but his is a Virginia first: It's located at a winery. And a very good one, at that.

Jim's wife Lori has long been synonymous with the local wine industry, producing award winners using traditional methods at the family's farm in Waterford, where she operates **Corcoran Vineyards**. And as passionate as she is about wine, Jim is about beer.

Perplexed by the lack of breweries in Virginia and yearning for a good beer close to home, he hired brew master Kevin Bills and hung out a shingle in 2012 – within stumbling distance of the vineyards.

Because the two immediately tapped the support of a larger brewing community, their fledgling effort was remarkably refined; it has continued to develop with experience and experimentation. The small brewery is open to the public on Saturdays and Sundays, dispensing a full line-up of beers along with a sound dose of optimism.

For a nominal fee you'll sample six brews; choices change with the season and may include Wheatland, P'ville Pale, Catoctin Ale, Corky's Irish Red, Slainte Stout, Paeonian Porter and Round Hill Root Ale. All are well balanced and flavorful, reflecting Jim Corcoran's motto: Great beer with LoCo attitude.

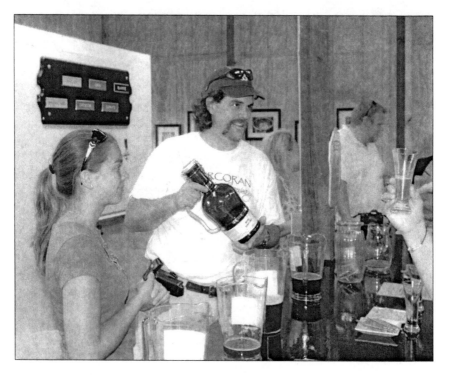

Kevin Bills turns out a lively selection of beers that are well received by the general public and the brewing community.

You can have a growler filled with your favorite beer to take home, and offerings are also available by the pint. The spot is a favorite with home brewers, who casually network in the tasting room and officially meet once a month for support and information from Bills and his assistant, Brian Spak.

If you're lucky, you'll experience the wit and wisdom of Jim Corcoran – it's his clubhouse, after all. Corcoran is a likeable, high-energy kind of guy who actively promotes agritourism (he's a former Chair of the Virginia Wine Council). Now that Jim has turned his attention to beer, he's stunned by the public's reaction; after just two weeks in business, he had to order more equipment to keep up with demand.

Meanwhile, back at the ranch … The small log-lined tasting room of Corcoran Vineyards is serving wines that are big on flavor – Traminette, Chambourcin, Cabernet Franc and Malbec, to name a few. And Corcoran Vineyards is one of the few wineries making apple wine, a crisp white that's perfect on warm summer days and pairs well with 'Q.

Monk's BBQ is here every weekend from mid-April to Thanksgiving, smoking up a storm of ribs, pulled pork, chicken, brisket and chorizo laced with handcrafted sauces that deftly incorporate Corcoran products.

The man behind the magic – Brian Jenkins – has been fine-tuning his recipes for 10 years now, and the effort shows in the sweet and tangy results. Brian started the fire back when the brewery opened, and after you visit him you'll wish he'd quit his day job, go whole hog and offer home delivery.

Monk's five-meat platter is a big seller, and ribs sell out quickly so stop by early in the day if you're planning on ordering them. A perennial favorite is the pulled pork sandwich, and sides of vinegar-based slaw and smoked beans consistently garner rave reviews.

Corcoran's Brewing Company is dog friendly and features a large patio for the beer crowd and picnic tables by a duckweed-covered pond for wine lovers. Virginia law dictates that never the two beverages shall meet, but visitors may enjoy their food in both venues.

The Corcorans have teamed up with JoAnne and Mike Carroll of the Leesburg Vintner to open the **Leesburg Brewing Company** (2 West Loudoun Street), a lively brewpub in the historic district of Loudoun's county seat. The American pub-food menu features handcrafted beer and Monk's BBQ, a match made in hog heaven.

Carpe Weekend's tip:

Monk offers a Thanksgiving turkey that's infused with a half-pound of Cajun butter, filled with cornbread and chorizo sausage stuffing and ready for pickup on Thanksgiving morning. His Christmas smoke includes whole pastrami, whole brisket, pork shoulder ham and turkey. Pre-order outrageously delicious holiday food by contacting Brian at MonksBBQ@gmail.com. Visit their website at www.MonksQ.com for a complete menu.

Next stop: the **Old Lucketts Store** (42350 Lucketts Road). You've probably noticed this long-standing landmark on Route 15 north of Leesburg, but this emporium is anything but a dusty old antique store.

Fabulous finds spill off a wraparound porch, and artfully arranged rooms full of bona fide antiques mingle with dried flowers and bins of keys, knobs, coat hooks – the stuff-of-life. The result is vintage hip, a happy salad that's so much more than the sum of its parts.

Neighboring **Beekeepers Cottage** specializes in romantic furnishings for the home, with a heavy dose of beads, baubles and trinkets. It's an easy, breezy place that lifts the spirits.

The barn near the Design House hints at the artfully arranged displays inside.

Pavilions in the yard showcase big, sturdy items like fireplace mantles, stained glass and outdoor statuary – the architectural elements that make a home a house – as well as the birdcages, old croquet sets and miniature greenhouses that make a house a home.

Every day the owners sell cool stuff at great prices, arranged in rooms that are fresh and full and ready to knock your socks off. But on the first weekend of every month, they go way over the top with the **Design House**.

Entry is made through a breezeway at the back of the property, where shoppers emerge in a courtyard that immediately spells fun. Step up into the house – breakfast pastries often await, along with steaming hot cups of coffee.

Suzanne Eblen and Amy Whyte are the creators of this place where old meets new and everything is reinvented in the process. They've coordinated room after room down to the finest detail, leaving you with the feeling that you must have it all.

Eblen explains that the two have a natural synergy and a good sense of humor, creating highly thematic and subtly entertaining rooms by concocting a detailed story for each one. She fondly recalls the evil stepsister room, with its twin beds strewn akimbo and decorating touches defying both conformity and peaceful coexistence.

The goal of Design House, in Eblin's words, is to provide a place where you can, "Come in, have fun and be happy." So when a customer admitted that she visited every month just to feel good, Eblen was delighted. Mission accomplished!

FYI:

- Enjoy this trip on the first weekend of the month (May – November).
- Corcoran Brewing Company opens on Saturdays and Sundays at noon.
- The brewery is pet friendly, inside and out.
- Corcoran Vineyards is open during the same hours.
- Visit individual websites for additional details.

The Heurich House is a masterpiece of craftsmanship and design, reflecting the eclectic taste of its owner.

Heurich House: A brewmaster's castle

The nation's capital is now a bonafide beer town; several microbreweries and gastropubs have come on the scene in recent months, dispensing every kind of suds imaginable. Even the White House brews its own. This day trip follows the trail of DC's love affair with beer, starting at the elegant Dupont Circle home of Christian Heurich.

Locals have dubbed it the **Brewmaster's Castle** (1307 New Hampshire Avenue NW), and it does, indeed, cast a massive and pleasantly incongruous shadow in Dupont Circle. Office buildings, embassies, residences and restaurants make this area a thriving enclave – and not exactly the place you'd expect to find a turn-of-the-century mansion built on the art of brewing.

But Dupont Circle has changed a bit since its development in 1871. At that time the Army Corps of Engineers began work in accordance with Pierre L'Enfant's plan, and during the decade that followed the area became a fashionable neighborhood for affluent Washingtonians.

Christian Heurich purchased the Schnell Brewery and Tavern at M and 20th Streets in 1872 and transformed it into the Christian Heurich Brewing Company, where he made beer and resided with his first wife, several employees and a servant. But when an explosion in the malt mill sparked a huge fire, he decided to build a fireproof mansion to call his own in the tony part of town.

Heurich's new Richardsonian Romanesque home was completed in 1894 and is now open to the public for tours and events. Heavy wood, mosaic tiles and faux finishes embellish rooms with 13-foot ceilings, and belongings reflect the German Baronial Renaissance taste of its owner.

When you enter the front hallway – replete with personal touches that include a full suit of armor – you instantly connect with Christian Heurich, a German immigrant who arrived in America with just $200 in his pocket to build a brewery and a legacy. This was a man who loved his family, his heritage and his beer.

A one-hour tour brings visitors through the mansion's formal rooms; the most elaborate is the front parlor, with ornate furniture and celestial ceiling decorations. A nearby music room with hand-carved interior musician's balcony makes it easy to imagine an evening of entertainment with the Heurichs.

Many of the original furnishings remain in gilded and glamorous settings.

Guests taking a meal in the heavily oaked dining room – surrounded by parquet floors and carved wooden walls, ceiling, mantle and furniture – may have been joined by Michael, a particularly creepy little doll that still resides on the sideboard. It's said that Mrs. Heurich enlisted Michael to take a seat at the table whenever a 14th guest was needed, lending insight on her superstitious nature.

You'll linger in a conservatory that's still gorgeous by today's standards, and continue upstairs to see graciously appointed bedrooms. But the most interesting part of the tour may just be the basement.

Here the bierstube is found, modeled after a German ale house. Its wooden centerpiece is adorned with hearty beer steins and carved with creatures ranging from the romantic to the grotesque. You half expect the well-endowed St. Pauli Girl to pop into the room, a sentiment shared by others on the tour. This was originally Heurich's man cave, and it later became the family's breakfast room.

The kitchen exudes a grand-yet-austere air, familiar to fans of Masterpiece Theatre's *Downton Abbey*. Communication tubes used by the servants reveal that Heurich enjoyed his technology, and many state-of-the-art systems are found in this turn-of-the-century home.

Central heating and cooling, an intercom and a burglar alarm – as well a fairly intimidating boiler room – are marvels of engineering. Most of the home's eight bathrooms are in their original condition, and its 15 fireplaces have never been used – perhaps the sign of a more-than-healthy respect for fire.

Heurich's new brewery opened in 1895, where the Kennedy Center now stands. It produced over 500,000 barrels of beer a year and survived Prohibition by garnering a contract to supply ice to both Congress and the Supreme Court.

At the time of his death in 1945, Heurich had become the world's oldest brewer. He departed this world at the age of 102 with words he lived by: Practice moderation and drink Heurich's beer.

Christian Heurich's final days are creatively imagined in *The Brewmaster's Castle*, a graphic novel by writer Matt Dembicki and cartoonist Andrew Cohen. Dembicki works nearby and was inspired after visiting the mansion and learning about its owner. The comic book is reasonably priced and makes a great souvenir of the day.

Note that on the third Thursday of every month, Heurich House hosts a History and Hops event from 6:30 to 8:30 p.m. Microbrewery owners are on hand to pour their beers, and tours of the mansion are given while musicians perform in the balcony.

The Heurich family enjoyed breakfast in the bierstube, surrounded by vintage beer steins and inspirational sayings on the topic of imbibing.

Fast forward to **Pizzeria Paradiso** (2003 P Street NW), this century's answer to the burning question: Where can we go for a cold one and a couple of slices?

Over 200 brews and a dozen or so drafts are served at the correct temperature in the proper barware, and Neapolitan-style pizzas are baked at 650 degrees in a wood-stoked oven that turns out some of the best pies in the city. Favorites include the Margherita, Atomica and Quattro Formaggio, with plenty of toppings to make them your way.

No discussion of DC's beer-story would be complete without mention of the Brickskeller. Known as a pioneer in the local craft beer movement, the Brick served up handcrafted, full-bodied brews as early as the 1970s to an adoring audience. It was once the epicenter of DC's beer culture, a distinction held for five decades.

Now some of the new kids in town – notably Birch and Barley and Meridian Pint – vie for that title, and the Brickskeller is no more. But you can get a glimpse of the past by visiting the **Bier Baron Tavern** (1523 22nd Street NW). It occupies the Brick's former building on what is still considered hallowed ground.

To truly experience this relic, bypass the Baron's newly renovated dining room and descend to the basement. The pub is a genuine hole-in-the-wall, an institution among the famous and infamous.

It's said that Aldrich Ames met Soviet operatives at the Brickskeller, and that then-owner Dave Alexander alerted authorities when he recognized Aldrich's photo from TV. Now the place has changed hands and the food's been upgraded, but the emphasis is still on great beer.

Fifty rare draft brews, numerous cask ales and over 500 bottled beers are offered from around the world, and a tasting fee gets you six short pours if you just can't decide. The Bier Baron is open into the wee hours on Fridays and Saturdays, so take your time.

FYI:

- Heurich House is closed during the month of January for maintenance.
- Tours are held on Thursdays, Fridays and Saturdays.
- Visit www.heurichhouse.org for hours and details.
- The closest Metro stop is Dupont Circle on the Red Line.
- On-street parking is limited, but several parking garages serve the area.
- Admission fee is modest, and National Trust members get discounts.

Carpe Weekend's tip:

Central Parking is found at 11 Dupont Circle (enter on New Hampshire Avenue). Discounted garage parking is available with a printed coupon, and you may obtain one at www.washingtondc.centralparking.com.

The flagship wine of Barboursville Vineyards is aged in the Octagon Room.

Barboursville Vineyards: Days of wine and ruins

If Thomas Jefferson were alive today, he would, no doubt, be pleased. Not necessarily with the state of the union, but certainly with the state of its wine industry.

A trip to Orange County's **Barboursville Vineyards** (17655 Winery Road) gives the visitor a look at our third president's dream – a thriving wine industry on American soil. Here one of Italy's most respected wine-making families is producing some of Virginia's most celebrated wines in the shadow of the ruins of one of Jefferson's finest architectural feats.

Enjoy a thought-provoking visit to all that remains of the mansion that Thomas Jefferson designed for Governor Barbour.

Jefferson loved the fruit of the vine; during his eight years in the White House, he spent approximately $16,500 on the European wines he uncorked to entertain guests and enlighten their palates. So it's not surprising that Virginia's most famous Renaissance man would want to give winemaking a try for himself.

Jefferson doggedly pursued the cultivation of *Vitis vinfera*, the classic European grape, for nearly a half century in his vineyards at Monticello in Charlottesville. He was convinced that, " We could in the United States, make as great a variety of wine as are made in Europe, not exactly of the same kinds but doubtless as good."

Despite Jefferson's passion for fine wine, he didn't produce a single glass. His nemesis – small but at that time unstoppable – was *Phylloxera vastatrix*, a species of aphid with a particular affinity for the roots of European vines.

Native American vines were naturally resistant to the pest but produced wines of inferior quality. Jefferson kept the hope alive that the young republic would one day give birth to fine wine, so he chronicled his attempts for future viticulturists.

In addition to having been a Founding Father, a prolific writer and a devoted wine enthusiast, Jefferson was also an accomplished architect. The house he designed in the early 19th century for his good friend and then-governor James Barbour was so spectacular that it came to be known as the finest residence in Orange County.

Construction of the masterpiece began in 1814 and continued for eight years, culminating in a work that incorporated Jefferson's trademark elements – most notably the octagonal great room. Barbour died in 1842, and the family continued to live there until fire destroyed the mansion on Christmas Day in 1884.

Meanwhile, things had finally started to look up for the Virginia wine industry. The war on bugs was won in 1877, thanks to the technology of grafting European vines onto American rootstocks to protect the fledgling plants from their mortal enemy.

About a century later the Zonin family, owners of the largest privately held wine company in Italy, made the fateful decision to expand to America; they chose to settle on the former Barbour estate. Just 20 miles north of Monticello and in the same valley, Barboursville Vineyards is now realizing Thomas Jefferson's dream.

For a small fee, visitors may try one of the largest tasting line-ups in Virginia

Winemaker Luca Pashina has guided this estate and influenced the leadership of Virginia viticulture for 20 years. The results of his progressive approach and creative outlook can be sampled in one of the most attractive tasting rooms in the Commonwealth.

The setting resembles an Italian farmhouse with stucco interior walls, exposed beam ceiling and ceramic tile floor. Compelling views of the surrounding countryside are framed by expansive windows, and it all resembles a folk art painting. A very classy one.

Tastings include over 15 wines, with your glass as a take-away souvenir. The bar is separated into three distinct stations – white, red and dessert wines – with a guru for each. This approach works perfectly for a winter visit, but traffic has been known to flow less smoothly in the busier months so it's best to arrive early.

Barboursville is Virginia's most elite winery, having earned four Governor's Cup awards since 1982, when the competition originated. It's 2009 Octagon is considered by some to be the best yet.

The gift shop is adjacent to the tasting room and sells accessories for the oenophile, as well as fine books on the topic. A tour of the winery includes the history of Barboursville and a visit to its stylish museum.

Exhibits offer a rare opportunity to commune with Thomas Jefferson and trace the path of his thought process, as he heeded the words of classic poet Virgil on tilling the earth. Sketches of Jefferson's plans for the orchards at Monticello are almost artistic.

In the winery's barrel room, row upon row of aging Octagon are stacked. This is Barboursville's flagship product, a Bordeaux-style blend of Merlot, Cabernet Franc, Cabernet Sauvignon and Petit Verdot that's worth the trip in itself.

A museum inside the winery displays antique equipment and details the evolution of wine making in Virginia.

Because Italians love their ruins, the Zonins decided not to restore the Barbour mansion but instead to stabilize it so that it wouldn't deteriorate any further. The scenic results are now on the National Register of Historic Places and open to the public daily; a self-guided tour is the perfect finish to the day.

FYI:

- The winery is open daily, with tours in the afternoon.
- The ruins are open until 5:30 p.m.
- Consult www.barboursvillewine.net for details.
- Picnic tables provide a great spot for a casual lunch with a view.
- The 1804 Inn at Barboursville Vineyards offers elegant lodging.
- Palladio Restaurant serves classic Northern Italian cuisine.
- Business casual attire is required for lunch and dinner.
- Reservations are required for dinner.

Carpe Weekend's tip:

The modest tasting fee includes an inscribed glass and entitles you to try 16-20 wines, several offered only at the winery. On subsequent visits, bring the souvenir glass and receive a discount on your tasting.

At the Blue Mountain Barrel House, Imperial Stout is aged in charred American bourbon barrels to create Dark Hollow.

Brew Ridge Trail: Not your father's Charlottesville

In the Blue Ridge Mountains of Virginia, everything seems to be found along a well-organized trail. The Wine Trail, the Artisan Trail and the granddaddy of them all – the Appalachian Trail – send us out in search of everything from the bounty of the land to inner peace.

And the Brew Ridge Trail? That gives us a place to kick back, relax, connect with one another and give thanks. The gifted few who brew are making a bit of magic here that may just border on religion, at least to the folks who congregate on their patios and decks and in the region's tasting rooms and biergartens.

This weekend-long romp will make you proud to be a Virginian, inspired by our talented brewers, their palatable products and the intoxicatingly beautiful countryside.

This hardware with heart dispenses Starr Hill's German-style hefeweizen, a local favorite.

At **Starr Hill Brewery** in Crozet (5391 3 Notch'd Road) you feel the love the minute you walk through the door. Maybe you've tried Jomo Lager, since any tap worth its suds dispenses this brew on occasion. But

Starr Hill also offers IPA, amber ale, pilsner, stout, seasonal beer and a German-style hefeweizen – affectionately labeled The Love – at their friendly-but-no-frills tasting room in an industrial facility in Crozet. I got a warm and fuzzy feeling the minute the train barreled through town and frothed up my beer.

Starr Hill is the recommended first stop on a Friday afternoon. It makes good sense, since you have to remain vertical to taste at the bar; plus, they close earlier than the other breweries. This is the place to enjoy a sampler and savor that first pint, shedding city slicker skin and chatting with the locals.

Wind down C'ville-style at **South Street Brewery** (106 W. South Street), just a block from Charlottesville's downtown mall. South Street Brewery offers an eclectic menu ranging from shrimp kebobs to big burgers, ribs and salads. The setting – in a renovated grain warehouse – is laid back and comfortable with brick walls, hardwood floors and hewn beams.

You may want to cozy up to the bar, since table servers can be preoccupied with the college crowd on Friday nights. Plus the bartenders are friendly and happy to dispense information about the area, along with what's on tap. Their Satan's Pony Amber Ale – a highly balanced blend of hops, malt and roasted flavors – makes the perfect nightcap.

Found in a former hay and grain warehouse, South Street Brewery is near Charlottesville's famous downtown mall.

Rise and shine with a visit to the **Barrel House** (495 Cooperative Way), Blue Mountain's new production facility in Arrington. It's recommended that you begin here on Saturday at 11 a.m. with a nice breakfast beer like Rockfish Wheat.

Which leads me to admit: I drank wheat beer. And I liked it.

I'm not particularly fond of a beer that's always unfiltered and usually smacks of banana taffy. But Rockfish Wheat and Blue Mountain's other beers – Kolsch 151, Uber Pils, Full Nelson IPA and the cask-conditioned Local Species and Dark Hollow – deftly avoid clichés while remaining true-to-form.

Beers are available to sample and by the glass, and tours of the impressive facility are held on weekends. You'll learn about their old-school parti-gyle system that creates a brother and sister beer from the same mash. It's unique to the region and draws home brewers and beer lovers from miles away. This tour's the most detailed and informative on the trail, so do arrive early.

Wild Wolf, serving up plenty of diversions, is a favorite with families.

With its biergarten, playground, ponds, water wheel and shopping village, **Wild Wolf Brewing Company** in Nellysford (2461 Rockfish Valley Highway) could easily win an award as the trail's most charming stop. Relaxing outside and enjoying a meal with the best of the Eagles wafting through the patio, you'll almost forget you're at a brewery.

But make no mistake: Brew Master Danny Wolf is crafting impressive beers behind his adorably rustic curtain. Wild Wolf Pils, Alpha Ale, Wee Heavy Ale and Black Wolf IBA (it's black, not pale) make up the menu of house beers, along with Blonde Hunny Ale that's had a little help from the bees at Hungry Hill Farm. Seasonal beers are also offered, and all brews reflect Wild Wolf's happy twist and creativity.

The main building – once a Nelson County high school – is cozy on fall days, and the converted tobacco barns host a village of boutiques. If you'd like to try your hand at the brewer's art, visit Libation for supplies. They'll set you up with everything you need.

Devils Backbone Brewing Company, located at the base of Wintergreen, is a lively stop in any season.

The sweeping vistas that surround **Devils Backbone Brewing Company** in Roseland (200 Mosbys Run) make this a fine destination at any time of day, but plan for an early evening arrival. As the sun sets and the patio lights come on, you'll have a sublime moment sipping Vienna Style Lager while taking in the rural surroundings.

Devils Backbone offers a full line of tradition-steeped favorites, including a pilsner, hefeweizen, IPA, wit bier, rye ale and their crowd-pleasing seasonal, the Ale of Fergus.

The interior of the building resembles a hunting lodge, complete with stonework crafted from local river rock. Moose, mountain goat and black bear heads peer over your shoulder as if to read the menu, which features organic vegetables and herbs that have been grown onsite.

Dine on Blue Mountain's patio or at the outdoor bar and enjoy veggie pizza with a view.

Blue Mountain Brewery's Afton restaurant (9519 Critzer's Shop Road) prepares its food from scratch – using local ingredients whenever possible – and grows the hops for Full Nelson IPA right on the property. A visit to the area isn't complete without sampling their gourmet pizza or choosing from an inspired menu that reflects the season.

Enjoy Sunday brunch at 11 a.m.; you'll appreciate a last chance to drink one of the superb beers you tasted at their Barrel House on Saturday, and to gaze out at the Blue Ridge Mountains.

The Boars Head in Charlottesville is set on 573 acres of idyllic Virginia countryside, offering photo opportunities and a place to unwind.

Who knew tasting beer could be so grueling? A return to base camp at the **Boar's Head** (200 Ednam Drive) in nearby Charlottesville provides the perfect recharge, with spa services that replenish and renew. Make appointments for massages, facials and beauty treatments – as well as soaks, wraps and other therapies – and enjoy the opportunity to detox and decompress in comfortable luxury.

The Boar's Head recently completed extensive renovations to their guest rooms, each creating a soothing environment with one of the most comfortable beds for miles around. The resort offers dining options that range from the romantic Old Mill Room, with elements from a 19th century gristmill, to the intimate Bistro 1834, with chairs you can sink right into. Craft beers are paired with signature dishes for an experience that's distinctly Charlottesville.

A weekend in Virginia's burgeoning beer country reveals an unexpected treasure: Handcrafted brews and innovative food in a farmland setting that'll knock your socks off. The laidback-yet-industrious vibe sends a clear message. Join us! This is how life can be! You'll want to sell the house, grab the dog, move to Nelson County and plant a hop farm. Or at least visit from time to time.

The Boars Head resort graciously combines Southern hospitality with fine dining, an award-winning golf course and athletic facilities.

FYI:

- This trip is best made on weekends, with a Friday evening arrival.
- Consult brewers' websites for hours, tours, dinners, music and events.
- Visit www.virginia.org/craftbeer to find additional breweries and restaurants serving craft beer.

Witness magic inside the famed motorcycle maker's modern assembly plant on its Steel Toe Tour.

2. OFF BEAT AND ON TOUR

Harley-Davidson Factory: Chrome-plated tour de force

It's said that four wheels move the body, but two wheels move the soul. I didn't really get the meaning of that until I took Harley-Davidson's Steel Toe Tour of its 650,000-square-foot vehicle operations plant in York, Pennsylvania.

Harley-Davidson employs state-of-the-art robotics and approximately 1,000 union workers in a streamlined process that turns out Touring, Softail, CVO and Trike models on a single, integrated assembly line and produces parts – frames, fuel tanks and fenders – for the legendary motorcycle maker.

In 2012 the York plant introduced its **Steel Toe Tour** (1425 Eden Road) as a direct result of an ongoing dialog between corporation and riders. Bikers have traditionally loved the factory's free one-hour tour, but they craved a more in-depth look at the manufacturing process. They wanted to witness firsthand the art of American-made steel being stamped, pressed, forged, formed, welded and dressed into the stuff of dreams.

The Steel Toe Tour is not for the faint of heart; it takes a full two hours, involves a hefty admission fee and leads visitors right out to the middle of the factory floor. But you'd be hard-pressed to find a better tour experience, a more interesting slice-of-life or a bigger dose of pride in American craftsmanship in under three hours of the nation's capital.

Small groups are outfitted in the requisite boots, protective eyewear and Hi-Vis vests before being guided past the perimeter and into another world, where the sights, sounds and smells of manufacturing surround. A laser-wielding robot takes aim to cut front fenders and drill bolt holes with precision, resembling a scene from Tony Stark's basement. The endeavor is a well-executed ballet of man and machine, with the line between the two often blurring.

Nowhere is this more evident than in the welding of the Touring frame. A human operator preps a 1,000-pound fixture and sends it into a gigantic cell, where robotic helpers are at-the-ready. The tight team of six welds and moves the fixture in a shower of sparks, completing 264 linear inches of welding in four minutes flat.

Stop by the Visitors Center, which features cycles in various stages of the production process.

Harley-Davidson pride is apparent, even in the smallest of details.

After it's returned to the human welder for inspection and touch-up, the frame and tail section go back to the cell to be placed on an exit conveyor. Frames are then loaded on a battery-powered driverless cart, which follows a magnetized strip on the floor and cues up for painting.

Particularly fascinating is a lesson on the powder-coating process, in which negatively charged paint powder is sprayed onto positively charged parts and then baked at 350 degrees Fahrenheit for 20 minutes, much like a cinnamon bun. Human touch-up artists take a trip through the wind tunnel – you can, too – and suit up to prevent dust and lint from lingering in the finished work.

Videos along the route explain parts of the process you can't see, but there's plenty to take in, all the same. Sparks fly, engines rev and the smell of paint hangs heavy in the air. Bruce Springsteen provides the soundtrack from a distant work station – I kid you not – competing with the din and just barely winning. As far as tours go, it really doesn't get much better than this.

A motorcycle is technically born in the USA when it gets stamped with a Vehicle Identification Number, at which point it enters the assembly line for its final journey. Remember the automated guided carts? The York plant employs a sizeable fleet and assigns one to carry each motorcycle on its entire trip through assembly. With all those driverless vehicles running around, it's imperative that visitors stay together, listen to the tour guide and obey the red-light-green-light system on the factory floor.

When the tour is over, you'll wonder where the two hours went. Even if you're not particularly into all things automotive, there's a certain level of patriotic pride in visiting a real live manufacturing facility that, while highly mechanized, has managed to keep a firm grip on its heart and soul.

FYI:

- The Steel Toe Tour is currently offered Monday – Thursday.
- Availability is limited, and reservations are available at 877-883-1450.
- Closed-toe, low-heeled shoes are required (no Crocs or clogs).
- Children under 12 are not permitted on factory tours.
- Visitors under 18 must be accompanied by an adult.
- Cameras, recording devices and large bags are not allowed.
- Admission includes a safety vest, commemorative pin and photo.
- Tours are not offered on major holidays or during production changes and year-end maintenance.

After touring the Harley-Davidson factory, why not go hog wild for lunch? **Appalachian Brewing Company** has several outposts in the area, and the one in Gettysburg 401 Buford Avenue) might be on the way for some travellers.

ABC is known for handcrafting beers with natural ingredients and a strict adherence to craft brewing standards. Flagship brews include Trail Blaze Organic Brown Ale, Water Gap Wheat, Purist Pale Ale, Mountain Lager, Jolly Scot Scottish Ale, Hoppy Trails IPA, Susquehanna Stout and a big, boozy Broad Street Barley Wine. Their menu includes salads, soups, sandwiches and full-size meals, with Mile-high Meatloaf and Brewer's Mac & Cheese weighing in as favorites.

But after a couple of hours watching Harley-Davidsons in production, you probably want to wrap your hands around the Hog Wild. This bad boy's been spanked with spices, braised in beer, slow roasted, dressed with root beer BBQ sauce and piled into a brioche roll.

The Hog Wild pairs perfectly with the Happy Trails IPA, providing the perfect fuel for riding off into the sunset.

Carpe Weekend's tip:

York County maintains a well-stocked Visitors Center inside the Harley-Davidson plant. Here you can get the free maps and brochures you'll need to continue your exploration of the self-proclaimed factory tour capital of the world.

Playful Antics was a prize winner in the 1998 Rose Parade, and now you can work the controls to see its polar bears romp in the snow.

Shenandoah Valley: Groovin' on a Saturday afternoon

One fine Saturday I explored the other Woodstock, traveled back in time through a covered bridge, stopped by a potato chip factory in the middle of nowhere and ended up at a warehouse full of funkadelic parade floats. At one point I seriously had to question the mushrooms I'd had on my pizza the night before.

By the time I got to Woodstock … I was very hungry. And a stop at the small Virginia town's **Woodstock Café** (117 S. Main Street) – known for yummy hot and cold beverages, breakfast pastries, egg sandwiches and an array of lunch foods – was positively groovy.

But first, the cinnamon roll. My flaky little friend.

I could go on forever about its yeasty goodness, its sticky-yet-not-too-sicky-sweet presence. For this reason, alone, I would recommend a detour off I-81 to Woodstock, Virginia. But don't miss the blackboard menu of other items – sandwiches, quiches, soups and salads.

The restaurant also stocks an eclectic collection of trinkets and decorative items – some from Ten Thousand Villages, supplier of fair trade items and purveyor of a certain peace-love-happiness vibe. And the Woodstock Café's wine shop is small but impressive, with several bottles boasting scores over 90 from the *Wine Spectator*.

Before rolling out of town, stroll Main Street and visit the **Farmhouse** (125 N. Main Street) for gourmet goodies and giftees to bring home, as well as **Three French Hens** (143 N. Main Street) for antiques with country flair.

Continue south on Route 11, where time appears to stand still, and over to the town of Mount Jackson. About one mile past the Shenandoah River crossing, take a right on Wissler Road to the 204-foot-long, single span **Meems Bottom Covered Bridge**.

The longest of Virginia's five preserved timber-covered bridges on public property, it effectively shuttled vehicles across the North Fork for 80 years – until vandals burned it down on Halloween of 1976. The bridge was rebuilt from salvaged timbers, with the addition of fire retardant materials for good measure.

You'll enjoy the same view that our 19th century counterparts did if you take just a few minutes to contemplate the ceiling. It has been restored to retain the intriguing geometric beauty of the original, and it looks just like the real McCoy.

The Meems Bottom Covered Bridge is the only timber-covered bridge maintained by VDOT as a traffic thoroughfare.

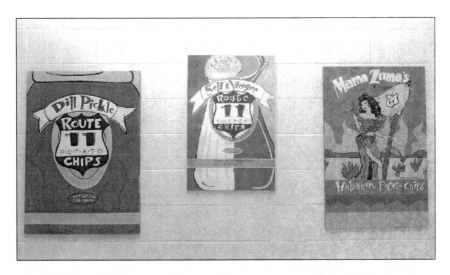

Route 11 Potato Chips come in many flavors, so everyone can find a favorite.

The folks at the **Route 11 Potato Chip Factory** (11 Edwards Way) have been among Virginia's premier micro-chippers for over 20 years. And while they've gained popularity over two decades, they still set a high priority on maintaining quality by producing America's favorite munchies in small batches.

Visit the company store – it's minutes from the covered bridge – for bags and tins of chips in a variety of flavors including barbeque, dill pickle, sour cream and chive, salt and vinegar, Chesapeake crab, sweet potato, Yukon gold and Mama Zuma's Revenge chips.

If you time it right, you'll get to see the entire production process – sans peeling – though huge windows. Keep in mind that if you're visiting specifically to view the frying action, it's best to call ahead (540-477-9664) to confirm the production schedule.

Earl Hargrove Jr. loves a parade. And lucky for us, he enjoys sharing that passion in the 40,000-square-foot warehouse he's dubbed **American Celebration on Parade** at **Shenandoah Caverns** (397 Caverns Road). Filled with nearly 30 of his favorite floats – spangly, sparkly works of art that tower over visitors in full, psychedelic glory – this museum and its treasures are anything but subtle. But there's more to these creative constructions than meets the eye.

The floats gathered here represent the collective pride we feel at the inauguration of our presidents, the celebration of our most important holidays and the coronation of our beauty queens. You feel the love the minute you walk through the door.

Larger-than-life animated polar bears frolic in snow banks, and a sea serpent tows King Neptune's chariot; both are veterans of Rose Parades held in Pasadena to celebrate the beginning of a new year. One of the most impressive pieces—a 30-foot-tall genie named *Three Wishes* – measures 47 feet from end to end and appears ready for your commands.

Many of the floats are interactive and some allow passengers onboard, so be sure to bring your camera to capture the moment. This is one museum that welcomes flash photography.

A Dixieland-style float features a banjo-playing pelican, as well as a clever cutaway that reveals the wizard behind the curtain. You'll learn a little about parade float technology and a lot about the company that's responsible for the whimsical worlds portrayed in the Rose Parade, the Miss America Parade and the Philadelphia Thanksgiving Day Parade.

Hargrove got his start decking department store windows in the 1940s, and now his company is proud to set the stage for trade shows and special events, including both the Republican and the Democratic National Conventions. This is a bipartisan party planner that knows how to roll out the red carpet.

One admission price gains access to American Celebration on Parade's floats, Main Street Yesteryear's department store windows, the Yellow Barn's tribute to farm life and Shenandoah Caverns' unique formations.

Kids love the Yellow Barn's indoor, working bee hive and the 35-foot-tall tree house that hosts a five-foot-tall family of squirrels. Parents love the wine tastings, as well as a sizable selection of microbrews and Virginia food products. The Yellow Barn hosts special events, including an Ozark Jubilee in the spring.

FYI:

- Woodstock Café is open daily.
- Route 11 Potato Chip Factory is closed on Sundays and holidays.
- Shenandoah Caverns is handicapped accessible.
- The combo ticket is discounted for AAA members, kids and seniors.
- A $2 coupon is available at www.shenandoahcaverns.com.
- Hours vary by season and attraction.

Carpe Weekend's tip:

If you plan to visit the caverns, be sure to bring a sweater or light jacket. The temperature is a fairly constant 56 degrees, year round.

Tranquility and beauty is found minutes from downtown Harrisonburg, Virginia, at the White Oak Lavender Farm.

White Oak Lavender Farm: A sea of tranquility

Day trippers of all ages escape the stress of everyday life with a visit to a working lavender farm. Beautiful countryside and mountain views clear the head, and a fresh, clean scent calms the soul. Children enjoy the menagerie of gentle barnyard animals, while Nana treasures the nearby Virginia Quilt Museum.

When you take a day trip to a farm, you need to eat like a farmer. And a visit to **Cristina's Café** (219 W. King Street) in downtown Strasburg, a quick detour off I-81, can certainly make that happen.

Breakfast is served every day and the kitchen – aka Cristina's Culinary Lab – turns out fabulous omelets and breakfast sandwiches from local free-range eggs, as well as fluffy pancakes made with natural ingredients. This is a healthy riff on stick-to-your-ribs comfort food.

A variety of platters are offered for a variety of reasons: The Mountain Man if you're very hungry, the Hangover if you partied a bit too hearty the night before and the Mexican if you like Mexican food. Lunch includes soups, sandwiches and café favorites such as empanadas and quiche.

The go-to beverage is coffee – espresso macchiato, café au lait and cappuccino, as well as bottomless cups of the strong, black stuff. It's fair trade, organic and delicious. And like any coffee house worth its beans, Cristina's features live music on Friday and Saturday nights.

A visit to **White Oak Lavender Farm** (5060 Newcomer Lane), on the outskirts of Harrisonburg, will lower your blood pressure and raise your spirits a notch or two. Here Julie and Rick Haushalter grow over 30 varieties of lavender and distill essential oils and florasol for use in their own line of bath, body, aromatherapy and culinary products.

A tour of the farm is inexpensive and departs from the gift shop, where a Zen-like tranquility fills the air along with heady scents and New Age music.

Julie guides visitors through fields and shares her farming philosophy and mission, educating us about the healing powers of this fragrant member of the mint family. Her portable still for steam extraction of the bud's essence is the only technology you'll see in a place where just about everything is done by hand.

It wouldn't be a farm without animals, and White Oak's menagerie is ridiculously cute. Alpacas, sheep and miniature horses share acreage with full-size equines, and Quest is almost famous because his grandsire was Triple Crown winner Secretariat. Kids are welcome to enter the Rabitat and cuddle Flemish Giants – not as scary as it sounds, since they're a docile breed of bunny.

The tour lasts about an hour and includes the opportunity to pick 20 stems of lavender, so you can bring that peaceful, easy feeling home with you. White Oak Lavender Farm's soaps, shampoos, lotions, aromatherapy oils and sachets are featured in the shop, along with live plants and edible lavender-infused items such as salt, pepper, sugar, tea and even chocolate.

A sign advises us to, "Keep calm and carry on," a popular bit from the 1939 British Ministry of Information. Julie explains, "Lavender can help us with that, allowing us to relax our bodies enough to find our coping skills." Ever in search of legal forms of relaxation, I left with a big bag of reasonably priced products and a newfound optimism.

Picnics may be eaten at tables with umbrellas near the Rabitat or on your own blanket near the duck pond. Lavender plants bloom in Virginia during June and July; call (540) 421-6345 before visiting for tour times and an update on the status of the buds.

Civil War history abounds in the Shenandoah Valley. The Battle of Cross Keys was fought directly across the street from White Oak Lavender Farm, and the property was used as a Union camp.

Numerous buildings in the area survived the fighting, and one is the Warren-Sipe House in downtown Harrisonburg, currently home to the **Virginia Quilt Museum** (301 S. Main Street).

Designated the official quilt museum of the Commonwealth, its 9,000 square feet offer an opportunity to learn about the fine art of quilting and see examples of work by both traditional and contemporary artists.

Special exhibits are presented, and the museum holds tea parties three times a year. A limited number of tickets for tea are usually available and may be reserved by calling (540) 433-3818.

Activities for children are scattered throughout the museum, and a gift shop on the first floor features quilting books, patterns, ornaments, cards, mugs and jewelry for the quilters in your life. Or, better yet, just bring them by for a visit.

FYI:

- This trip is best made in June or July, when lavender is in bloom.
- To enjoy all the elements, visit on a Saturday.
- Cristina's Café is closed on Tuesdays and Wednesdays.
- Tours of White Oak Lavender Farm are offered daily for a small fee.
- Visit www.whiteoaklavender.com for details about tours and classes.
- There is a small fee for admission to the Virginia Quilt Museum.
- The museum is closed on Sundays, Mondays and major holidays.

Fantasy Farm hosts an amusing assortment of colossal collectables, proudly
displayed by owner George Farnham.

West Virginia: Weird and wonderful

This journey takes us to an endearing Morgan County town with two names: Berkeley Springs and Bath. Similarly, the area has two entirely different personalities – one grounded in history, the other sublimely irreverent and zoning-free.

First, the modern marvel that is **Fantasy Farm** (14633 Winchester Grade Road). In the rolling countryside of West Virginia's Eastern Panhandle, George Farnham's happy acreage is a classic example of collecting gone amuck in a world without rules. Suffice it to say that this guy has probably never colored within the lines.

You're welcome to stop by his place in Unger – a rural outpost that redefines the middle of nowhere – to see for yourself. And, if you're lucky, you'll get to meet this quirky curator of the colossal. His farm is a breath of fresh air for those of us who live in tasteful subdivisions.

Life as George Farnham knew it changed forever when his wife, Pam, gave him a 25-foot tall fiberglass Muffler Man for his 50th birthday, several years ago. Smitten by the new hobby, the couple soon added Brian the beach dude, Big John the grocery store bag boy and a hamburger man with a sandwich so big it would make Guy Fieri drool.

A particularly prized addition is the Uniroyal Gal, a bikini-clad giantess with clip-on clothing for more modest climes. The collection also features a welcoming committee of Yogi Bear's cohorts, a 165-foot, non-operational rollercoaster with its cargo of Simpsons and a Paul Bunyan that recalls a famous scene from the movie *Fargo*.

These fiberglass behemoths were once used as eye-catching advertisements, tripling business along the highways of America in the early 1960s. Farnham, a wheeler-dealer on eBay, has assembled the largest collection to be found on private property to date.

Fantasy Farm has not been without its 15 minutes of fame. The folks at the website *Roadside America* have dubbed it Farnham Colossi, and in 2011 an independent film maker tried – but failed – to raise funds to feature it in a documentary about fiberglass collectors across the country.

Farnham remains humble about his accomplishments, explaining that living in a place with no zoning requirements gives him a unique opportunity to share his collection with the public. "The neighbors like it, too," he points out, "Since the UPS guy hardly ever gets lost now."

GPS can get a little wonky out here, so just travel south on Route 522 out of Berkley Springs for two miles to Winchester Grade Road. Continue on for 14 miles and turn left at the Unger Store. Go a mile and a half to the big Santa Claus in front of the purple barn – honestly, you can't miss it.

The five-acre **Berkeley Springs State Park** (2 S. Washington Street) is the centerpiece of the town formally known as Bath, appropriately boasting a unique monument to presidential bathing.

The Roman Bath House was built in 1815, making it the oldest public building in Berkeley Springs.

George Washington's Bathtub is a must-see in
Berkeley Springs State Park.

Our first president actually did partake of the "fam'd Warm Springs" for
their medicinal powers. But while he never actually used **George
Washington's Bath Tub** (it was constructed in 1930), Washington did
enjoy the same springs in approximately the same place. And it's still a
bubbling source of nearly 1,500 gallons of sparking clean water per
minute with a constant temperature of 74 degrees, same as it ever was.

You, too, can take the 102-degree waters in one of two historic buildings:
The circa 1929 yellow brick Main Bathhouse or the 1815 Federal style
Roman Bath House. Reservations are required by calling (304) 258-
2711.

The Museum of the Berkeley Springs is located on the second floor of the Roman Bath House and features photos of the way things were, along with a fetching display of woolen bathing apparel. You can bring home a free souvenir by bringing containers and filling them with Berkley Springs' finest in the adjacent Gentlemen's Spring House.

Pick up brochures for restaurants, shops, lodging, arts and culture, private spas and a historic walking tour in one of the bath houses or at the **Berkeley Springs Visitors Center** (127 Fairfax Street). Antique stores abound, and the two largest emporiums are the **Berkeley Springs Antique Mall** (7 Fairfax Street) and the **Old Factory Antique Mall** (282 Williams Street).

Specialty stores sell niche items, with **Retrodini** (81A N. Washington Street) paying homage to the 1940s through the 1980s. It's worth a stop to experience the Don-Draperesque vibe. **The Vintage Kitchen** (110 S. Green Street) offers old china and cottage style finds, as well as linens, cards and stuffed bears.

East of town on Route 9 **Youngblood's Antiques** (944 Martinsburg Road), is a purveyor of furniture both old and new, along with the best selection of statuary and garden gnomes available for miles around (although none of Lewis Youngblood's lawn ornaments quite rival those at George Farnham's Fantasy Farm).

You may find the owner at his antique cash register ringing up sales of collectibles as well as fine Amish reproduction furniture, jams, leather goods and the love-'em-or-hate-'em gnomes.

There are plenty of places to grab food on the fly – the **Fairfax Coffee House** (23 Fairfax Street), **Earthdog Café** (398 S. Washington Street) and **Creekside Creamery** (123 Congress Street) – and several restaurants that offer innovative dining in an interesting setting.

Lot 12 Public House (117 Warren Street) is a local go-to spot for an upscale dinner in a casually elegant atmosphere – the Farnhams were engaged here. And the view from **Panorama at the Peak** on Route 9 west of town is breathtaking, while their menu includes local, organic and some vegetarian choices. Reservations are recommended at these two restaurants.

FYI:

- Like much roadside art, Fantasy Farm has no set hours of operation.
- George Farnham tends to pop out of his house when visitors arrive.
- The Berkley Springs Bath House is closed on major holidays.
- The Creekside Creamery is closed on Tuesdays.
- Visit www.berkleyspringssp.com for information about baths, massages and sauna treatments.

Carpe Weekend's tip:

Make reservations if you'd like to dine at Lot 12 Public House or Panorama at the Peak. Both are closed on Mondays, Tuesdays and Wednesdays, and Lot 12 is also closed in January. Panorama at the Peak serves lunch and dinner, while Lot 12 is for dinner only.

Daring wing walkers entertain weekend crowds at the Flying Circus.

The Flying Circus Airshow: On a wing with a prayer

This Fido-friendly day trip to Virginia's Fauquier County brings families back to the good old days with humor, historic hijinks and heart-pounding suspense.

How many flight attendants can talk you through turbulence, check your carry-on bags and hop out on the wing to remedy technical difficulties?

Jana Leigh McWhorter ran off to join Bealeton's **Flying Circus** (5114 Richie Road) several years ago, and she's been one of its star attractions ever since. On weekdays she ensures the safety and comfort of her passengers on a small commercial aircraft, resisting temptation and keeping her feet firmly planted inside the aircraft. But weekends are an entirely different story.

Jana is a wing walker, one of a lively crew of aviators who've made it their mission to re-enact the great barnstorming days of the 1930s on a bucolic 200-acre park in Fauquier County, just one hour – but decades away – from the nation's capital.

This, ladies and gentlemen, is a living history lesson. A heart-pounding, gut-wrenching, schmaltzy salute to the past.

Every Sunday from May through October the gates open at 11 a.m., and the show starts promptly at 2:30 p.m. with a rousing rendition of the Star Spangled Banner. Pilots in antique flying machines perform feats of derring-do, cruising at low altitude, grouping in tight formation and re-enacting skits that made barnstorming popular between World War I and World War II.

The announcer laces humor with history, turning the day into one big patriotic smile that will send you home googling the glory days of aviation. A laid-back feeling accompanies aeronautical antics, and the audience chuckles as a biplane drops flour bombs on outhouse-bound Black Baron. Similar shtick ensues.

The Flying Circus offers an action-packed afternoon with a nostalgic look at the early days of aviation.

But the mood suddenly shifts when our wing walker of the day takes to the air, sharing a vintage biplane with her pilot. And, at just 200 feet above the ground and 80 miles per hour, she gracefully steps out onto the wing. Without a net. Or a 'chute.

The audience lets out a collective gasp, and there is complete silence as the plane makes an upside-down loop. Thoughts swirl through my head: Jana Leigh McWhorter! Get in that plane this instant! OMG, can I breathe yet?

Apparently not. Our daredevil defies both gravity and death, dangling by what must be the strongest ankles in Virginia. When the plane finally lands and heartbeats return to normal, the gates to the airfield swing open and we're all invited to meet the performers.

History buffs appreciate this rare opportunity to see meticulously restored antique planes up close, while kids swarm the pilots and wing walker seeking autographs for posters. Personally I was just glad that everyone was on the ground, safe and sound.

To make the most of your visit to the Flying Circus, arrive at 11 a.m. and enjoy old-timey radio broadcasts featuring big-band-era music and historic news stories. Ads for exciting new products like the state-of-the-art Studebaker contribute to the ambiance.

Norton, my Goldendoodle puppy, enjoys the
shade of classic aircraft after the show.

Set up a picnic spread and visit the gift shop to book a plane ride for before or after the show. Trips range in intensity and price, from a single-passenger piper cub cruise to a white-knuckle biplane ride. Passengers must be 16 or older to take the aerobatic version, which includes a turn spin, loop, roll and hammerhead.

While the pilots may stage a few dog fights, the Flying Circus is actually Fido-friendly, as long as pets are well behaved and on leashes. I brought a big water dish for Norton, because it gets hot out in the sun and furry friends need to stay hydrated. Refills are available in the restrooms, as well as from the spigot behind the snack bar.

Human companions may want to try the snack bar's other offerings, including snow cones, floats, cheeseburgers, pork BBQ, nachos, frozen candy bars, beverages and, occasionally, lemon meringue pie – a fitting dessert for a day that celebrates the past.

Annual themed shows include a Motorcycle Day with half-price admission for motorcycle riders, and a Hot Air Balloon Festival in August. The final show of the season is in late October.

Just a quick detour south down Route 28 in Remington is the **Moo-Thru** (11402 James Madison Highway). Hand-dipped scoops are served up on homemade waffle cones, in addition to root beer floats, banana splits, milk shakes and sundaes.

The Moo-Thru in Remington is a refreshing stop on this trip to the country.

This is real ice cream made by real dairy farmers from happy Holsteins that graze along the river, just a mile away. Flavors include Blackberry,

Blue Angel and my personal favorite, Mounds Bar. The Moo-Thru is open every day of the week.

Covered outdoor picnic tables make the Moo-Thru dog-friendly, and the house special is a Pup Cup – vanilla ice cream with two milk bones on top – for just $1. Country music plays while the kids get their ice cream fix and the dog slurps up his treat. 'Nuff said.

FYI:

- The Flying Circus performs on Sundays from May – October.
- Admission price varies by age.
- Several picnic tables are found beyond the parking area.
- Bench seating is provided, and you're welcome to bring stadium cushions, fold-up chairs and blankets.

Carpe Weekend's tip:

A $2 discount coupon is often offered at www.flyingcircusairshow.com.

A crystal-clear pool inside the Luray Caverns makes it tough to tell where the real thing ends and the reflection begins.

Luray Caverns: Journey to the center of the earth

It's said that you shouldn't take life too seriously – you'll never get out alive – and that's the inspiration for this trip. The day begins with a table of strangers at an award-winning bakery, features a subterranean tourist trap and ends at the best little bar in Front Royal, Virginia.

Our first stop is the **Red Truck Bakery** (22 Waterloo Street) in Warrenton. Grab one of their sweet or savory pastries and head for the communal table, found by sniffing the scent of cinnamon that wafts from the kitchen. Then pull up a chair and meet the random collection of folks who gather here to break bread.

It had been a year since my last visit and, amazingly, the only Warrenton resident I know happened to wander in. Then we were joined by an Alexandria native who shared local lore that's bound to show up in another story on another day.

That's what it's like at the Red Truck. You never know who you're gonna meet, but you do know what you're gonna eat: Perfectly prepared muffins, scones and croissants accompanied by the finest high-octane brew around, apropos of a bakery found in a circa 1921 Esso station.

After breakfast hop on Route 211 to **Luray Caverns**, the largest and most popular caverns in the East. This National Landmark is the big cajuna of caves.

On August 13, 1878 Andrew Campbell made the discovery of the century when he caught a cool breeze escaping from a gap in the limestone earth. He proceeded to crawl into a natural wonder that now lures families and field trips 150 feet under the earth's surface.

The Red Truck Bakery is known for its pastries, pies and double-chocolate moonshine cake.

Luray Caverns is an essential destination for anyone who claims to be a Virginian, whether transplanted here or native to the land. If you go on a weekend, arrive early in the day to avoid the crowd. And it certainly doesn't hurt to make friends with your fellow spelunkers, who can provide a wealth of information.

The tour covers over one mile and takes about an hour. High points include the 7-million-year-old *Big Shaggy*, a flowstone work of Mother Nature that's 40-feet tall and 120 feet in circumference, and *Fried Eggs* that look real enough to eat. While some of the formations have official monikers, it's more fun to make up your own.

Kids are definitely worth listening to, even if you don't bring any of your own. The naming committee ahead of us skipped along, declaring, "Look, it's Mickey Mouse … It's a bad guy's brain … It's my mother's Uncle Frank!"

Luray Caverns is home to the world's largest natural musical instrument, the Stalacpipe Organ. Invented by Leland Sprinkle in 1957, the organ uses mallets that strike formations to make the rocks sing. The chamber is a popular wedding venue – over 500 couples have been hitched here.

You'll exit through a gift shop that features the usual suspects – tee shirts, shot glasses and jewelry – and a few things probably not found in your town or even in your decade. Old timey toy shotguns and corn cob dolls remind us that we're at one of the region's oldest attractions, still thriving after all these years.

On the same property, the **Car and Carriage Caravan** displays over 140 vehicles end-to-end, creating one, big, anachronistic traffic jam. Notable are an 1840 Conestoga wagon, a 1927 Bugatti and a 1910 Model T that retailed for $550 when it was new. There's another gift emporium here, in case you've failed to fully empty your wallet.

This 1928 Packard pays tribute to the history of transportation in the Car and Carriage Caravan.

The **Luray Valley Museum** chronicles the history of the region in a much more peaceful setting than the previous two attractions, providing a tasteful diversion on a day that's all about kitschy fun. An array of cast iron stoves, pots and washboards recalls the mining days of the 1800s, and a collection of furniture and pottery showcases the craftsmanship of the valley. Spinning wheels, butter churns and other stuff-of-rural-life give a glimpse of local residents who were hard workers and handcrafters.

The **Garden Maze** is an ornamental garden with eight-foot-tall hedges that's probably best left until the end of the day. Visitors are treated to a cooling mist while navigating through an acre that's right out of *The Shining*.

When you've exhausted yourself and all of the possibilities, hop back on the highway to the **Lucky Star Lounge** (205A E. Main Street) in Front Royal for dinner. You'll thank your lucky stars you did.

The Lucky Star Lounge is a bar. A very wonderful bar.

If the kids are with you, the tables on the floor are the way to go. But if they're not, cozy up to the bar and hang out with owner Trevor Lipton and talented bartender Tim. They'll keep a steady stream of plates and drinks coming, spiced with witty conversation and an energetic vibe.

Don't usually sit up at the bar? But today we are on an adventure, not taking life too seriously and all, right? Besides, this is the bar you've been waiting for, the one with great food, colorful locals and an English bloke who makes you laugh.

Meals are fairly healthy and prepared to order with ingredients gathered from the local farmers market. Feeling wild and crazy, I let Trevor select my food and Tim pick my drink for me.

Trevor's house special – roasted salmon with heirloom tomatoes and fresh lemon basil over apple and thyme flavored rice – was quite tasty and probably would have paired well with a variety of beverages. Tim selected the Delirium Tremens pale ale from Belgium, a real winner.

These guys know their hops and malts. Trevor hails from London, and several times throughout the evening he was heard exclaiming, "Gawd, I love beer!" to no one in particular. Taps dispense brews and microbrews, and bottles are a respectable lot, as well. But be forewarned: The Lucky Star is a Bud-free zone.

Live music is featured every night in a variety of musical stylings, and on Saturdays the band sets up at 9:30 p.m. for a jolly good time. Regulars call ahead to reserve their favorite seats, so come in early if you plan to end your day trip by rocking into the night.

FYI:

- The Red Truck Bakery and Lucky Star Lounge are closed on Sundays.
- Luray Caverns is open every day of the year.
- Admission fee for the caverns varies by age.
- Visit www.luraycaverns.com for additional information.
- Temperatures underground hover at 54 degrees, so bring a sweater.
- The pathway is paved to accommodate wheelchairs and strollers.

Carpe Weekend's tip:

Luray Caverns Discovery Day is held every August, featuring a candlelight tour and costumed interpreters during the day and fireworks in the evening. Visit www.luraycaverns.com for details.

The museum's iconic whirligig, *Life, Liberty and the Pursuit of Happiness* by Vollis Simpson, is on permanent display in the courtyard.

Elaine C. Jean

American Visionary Art Museum: A cure for the blues

It's said that laughter is contagious, and maybe that's why visitors emerge from the American Visionary Art Museum in Baltimore a bit giddy. Charm City is big on fun these days, and this inspired museum at the base of Federal Hill might just be party central.

You'll feel the joy the minute the **American Visionary Art Museum** (800 Key Highway) comes into sight – all spangly and happy, adorned with glass pieces and mirror shards that catch the sun's rays and bounce them in every direction. Or maybe it's the three-ton whirligig that clues you in. Nadya Volicer's welcome mat in the foyer invites you to *Smile* – it's embedded with approximately 1,500 toothbrushes. Pretty soon, you won't have to be asked.

Artwork featured at the AVAM has been created by ordinary people ranging from high school dropouts to accomplished attorneys – WWII veterans and conscientious objectors alike – using hubcaps, electronic parts and other stuff of life, as well as glitter glue, poster paint, milk cartons and even drugstore cosmetics. Oh, and sometimes the iridescent wings shed by a certain Thai beetle.

Some of the artists are society's scavengers: Dumpster divers and hoarders living off the grid, on the wagon or in the apartment building next door. Most don't have formal training, but all have answered an inner call to create. You'll soon realize that these folks are anything but ordinary, and their art is genuine.

This is one museum where I break my adult-self rule and visit the gift shop first. The truth is, I usually visit the **Sideshow** twice – once upon entering the museum, and again before leaving the main building. It's just that good.

The Sideshow's motto is, "Come shopping, leave smiling."

The Sideshow sells original artwork and great books, as well as fun jewelry made from used paint brushes, old buttons, petrified bugs and the usual bling. Their collection of nostalgic toys and off-beat novelties is enough to make Archie McPhee green with envy. Inflatable turkey? Check. Chicken-shaped purse? Got it. Two-headed alien baby doll? Yours for just $25.

A genuine Zoltar fortune teller presides over the front of the store, dispensing prophesies that you may just begin to believe. The store's motto is, "Come shopping, leave smiling," and I always do.

The museum's permanent collection room on the first floor provides an abrupt shift in gears and includes the work of Paul Darmafall – the Baltimore Glassman – as well as an enormous model of the Lusitania built from 196,000 toothpicks and five gallons of glue by Wayne Kuzy. Of his herculean feat the artist once said, "It's a challenge. There's a lot of people who like to climb mountains like Mount Everest ... I choose to build models. It's safer."

A biography of each artist accompanies the work. The stories are pointed and poignant, often describing the triumph of the human spirit over adversity – disability, addiction, mental illness or hard times. In other cases, they tell of the happy conclusion to a life well lived. When viewed alongside each creation, a bigger picture emerges; in a sense, the entire museum feels like one grand work of art.

Revolving exhibitions are featured on the second floor and change annually. Past themes have included *What Makes Us Smile*, *All Things Round: Galaxies, Eyeballs and Karma* and, most recently, *Lies, Enchantment, Humor and Truth*. The common thread is often the irony of the human condition.

The banister of the main staircase is bedazzled with bottle caps and bling, and often its walls showcase confessions collected by Frank Warren, the creator of *PostSecrets*. Warren is a member of the AVAM's advisory board, along with medical rights activist and clown-for-peace Patch Adams and Baltimore filmmaker and artist John Waters.

Fifi is the mascot of the Kinetic Sculpture Race, where entries are human-powered works of art that traverse 15 miles of asphalt, mud and the waters of the Inner Harbor.

Patty Kuzbida's *What, Me Worry?* bed – paying homage to Alfred E. Newman with glass beads, found jewelry, and the farmed wings of the aforementioned Thai beetle – has been included in more than one exhibition, and if you're lucky it will be featured when you visit.

Across the courtyard in the **Jim Rouse Visionary Center**, the Cabaret Mechanical Theatre is an unusual collection of interactive wooden sculptures. The diminutive decorations never fail to delight – or appall – with titles including *Dustomatic* by Keith Newstand and *Flogging a Dead Horse* by Paul Spooner. Viewers push buttons and set structures in motion, witnessing that the devil is often in the details.

Sharing the gallery and not to be missed is DeVon Smith's enchantingly humanesque *World's First Family of Robots*. Smith – a WWII veteran who made his living as a junk dealer and trader – held the Guinness World Record for having hitchhiked over 500,000 miles in his lifetime.

DeVon Smith left us with the words he lived by: Don't sit in a chair. Get out and do it.

Yes, get out and do it. Hop in the car, blast up to Baltimore and spend a day at the AVAM; it really will make you smile. But it will also make you think and feel. And that's what great art is supposed to do, isn't it?

FYI:

- The AVAM is open Tuesday – Sunday (closed Mondays).
- Admission fee varies by age.
- Metered parking is available on Covington Street and Key Highway.
- The museum is handicapped accessible.
- The museum is open and admission is free on MLK Day.
- Visit www.avam.org for additional information.
- The Tall Structure Barn and Wildflower Garden are open air, and public art abounds.

Carpe Weekend's tip:

Fine dining is offered at the museum's Mr. Rain's Fun House, with a season-sensitive menu complimented by innovative cocktails, artisanal wines and craft beers.

The American Visionary Art Museum is proud to host **Baltimore's Almost Famous Annual East Coast National Championship Kinetic Sculpture Race**, usually held in the month of May.

It's a race of wacky, imaginative and totally human-powered works of art that have been designed to travel on land, through mud and over deep harbor waters. Crafted of backyard junk and garage cast-offs, machines are piloted by kinetinauts vying for the coveted title of Grand Mediocre East Coast Champion – finishing smack in the middle of the pack.

AVAM invites spectators to line the 15-mile race course through Baltimore and watch amphibious works of art fly by. And, of course, AVAM welcomes all entries, great and small.

While visiting the museum, I caught up with Founder and Director Rebecca Alban Hoffberger in the Jim Rouse Visionary Art Center. She proudly steered me over to see Fifi – a race mascot and previous winner of the Next to Last Award – explaining that this is a race unlike any other on the East Coast. It's more about the celebration of ingenuity and creativity than it is about the actual competition.

"Come early for the Blessing of De Feet," Dame Rebecca advises, "and you really should bring bribes for the judges – chocolate chip cookies, or something like that. We want to teach kids how the real world works."

A dockside view along the west coast of the Chesapeake Bay sets the tone for the day.

3. A LITTLE R & R

Southern Maryland: Sitting on the dock by the bay

A day trip to the west coast of the Chesapeake Bay offers a great escape within an hour's drive of the Metro area. Once you settle in with a tropical drink, you'll feel like you've been on vacation all week. And best of all, you won't have to cross the Bay Bridge or sit in traffic to get there.

If you're a beach bum who's short on time, short on funds or short on gas, chart your course for the **Chesapeake Beach Resort and Spa** (4165 Mears Avenue) in the town of Chesapeake Beach. Here you can park for free and walk to surrounding attractions, getting your lay of the land at the tiny but charming **Chesapeake Beach Railway Museum**.

Housed in an old railroad station, the museum highlights the intertwined histories of two romantic beach towns that grew up around the Washington and Chesapeake Railway Company's lavish resort. Woolen swim suits, antique souvenirs and a scale model of the waterfront amusement district bring into focus a bygone era.

By the beginning of the 20th century, people arrived by train and steamboat to enjoy the mile-long pier and grand boardwalk – featuring a bowling alley, band shell, games of chance, casino and even dancing bears. A spectacular addition, the Great Derby rollercoaster was built over the water in 1915.

The Chesapeake Beach Hotel and Spa offers services and events to enjoy during a day at the Bay.

Hurricanes, fires, and the Depression spelled doom for the development, and the dream of a park to rival Coney Island was pretty much over by 1935. But while the amusements are long gone, nostalgia lingers in everything from the architecture to the seafood. And there are plenty of activities for people of all ages and interests to enjoy.

Today's Chesapeake Beach Resort and Spa is reminiscent of many of the grand old beach resorts of the Mid-Atlantic. It boasts two marinas with charter fishing excursions and transient boat slips, a day spa that offers pampering massage therapy and three appealing restaurants – the **Rod 'N' Reel**, **Smokey Joe's Grill** and the **Boardwalk Café**.

The latter is perched right on the water, and it's a particularly good place to grab some appetizers and a fru-fru drink – because nothing says vacation day like a beverage packed with fruit and rum with an umbrella on top. If the family wants more excitement, ask anyone at the hotel for directions to **Brownie's Beach** for ancient shark tooth hunting or visit the **Chesapeake Beach Water Park** across the street for plenty of fun in the sun.

For a mere two bits, you can hop the **Beach Trolley** to nearby North Beach for a whole 'nother experience. A thriving community of summer cottages back in the day, its residents enjoyed the amusements of Chesapeake Beach along with a few casinos of their own.

Now a half-mile long boardwalk is the centerpiece of the town, alongside a petite strand of beach with a Visitors Center that offers everything you need to make your day at the Bay a success. Bike and boat rentals? Check. Umbrellas and chairs? Ditto that. North Beach may be small, but it has all the amenities of the big guys.

One block from the beach is the **Bay Avenue Shopping District**, with unique establishments that offer ice cream cones, old fashioned candy and the necessary beach supplies. Two antique stores, an award winning bakery, an eclectic gift shop, a local history museum, several restaurants and a wine store round out the choices.

Turn-of-the-century beach lovers once arrived at the town's train station, which is now a quaint museum.

The sand and surf at North Beach offer a slice of seaside life just one hour from Washington, DC.

North Beach charges admission to the sand and sells fishing and crabbing permits – with some luck, you may even catch dinner. If the fish aren't biting, just drive over to the dockside bar at **Skipper's Pier** (6158 Drum Point Road) in Deale and feast on the local fare.

Skipper's has traditionally received a slew of awards from Chesapeake Bay Magazine for some of the best oysters, crab cakes and steamed crabs around. New management has added a reasonably priced Sunday Brunch in addition to the full breakfast menu. But while you might come for the seafood, you'll stay for the views. And the Malibu Black Painkillers.

On a recent visit I saw a boat pull up to the dock, unloading its catch and delivering crabs right to the kitchen. Ours tasted just that fresh. Sailboats and other pleasure craft slid past us out on Herring Bay and live music filled the air, along with the voices of our deck mates.

And for the remainder of the day, this was the only spot in the universe.

The steamed crabs at Skipper's Pier are some of the freshest and best in the area, and the view is tough to beat.

FYI:

- Admission to the museum is free.
- Admission to the Chesapeake Beach Water Park is reasonably priced.
- Access to Brownie's Beach is inexpensive, as is access to North Beach.
- North Beach fishing and crabbing permits are available for a small fee.
- Check websites for hours of operation.
- The Chesapeake Beach Railway Museum closes for the winter.

The Migyar Dorje Stupa is the focal point of Peace Park.

Kunzang Palyul Choling: Dharma near DC

Every once in a while it soothes the soul to step back and take a look at the bigger picture, so a visit to the nearby Tibetan Buddhist temple in Poolesville, Maryland makes a most pleasant day trip.

Escape the trappings of everyday life by hiking trails through Peace Park, enjoying the beauty of parrots and macaws in a large bird sanctuary and touring a temple that looks like it's from the other side of the world.

First of all, know that everyone is welcome at **Kunzang Palyul Choling**'s 72-acre campus (18400 River Road) – one of the largest communities of ordained practitioners of Buddhism in the country. Buddhism is not a religion of conversion so KPC is a spiritual haven for everyone, including the casual day tripper.

KPC was founded by Jetsunma Ahkon Lhama – nee Alice Louise Zeoli – of Brooklyn, NY. She is the first Western woman to be recognized as Tulka, or reincarnate Lama and lineage holder, in the Tibetan Buddhist tradition. Jetsunma is an honorific title associated with Tara – the female Buddha who nurtures, protects and cares for all living beings with boundless compassion.

While many of the rituals and adornments you see here may be new to you, there's a vibe of comfort and familiarity that starts when you pull into the parking lot amid bumper stickers that encourage you to *Visualize Whirled Peas, Practice Random Acts of Kindness* and *Free Tibet.*

The feeling continues when you step up to the door of the roomy colonial house in rural Montgomery County. But on the other side, another world awaits. A peaceful, welcoming, orderly world. The setting is ideal for this brand of Buddhism that bridges the ancient wisdom of Tibet with the contemporary mind of the West.

The **Dharma Room** is the educational center, featuring a large sand mandala, two elaborate teaching thrones and several altars, as well as richly colored tonkas – traditional paintings on silk – and numerous sacred texts. The visual impact is dramatic, instantly dashing my preconceived notion of monastic, Zen-like simplicity.

The room is home to an enormous collection of crystals, nature's gems that represent the natural mind with no distractions. The crystals are another example of East-meets-West in this place that seeks to inspire people to improve the world and bring an end to the suffering of all sentient beings.

Nowhere is this mission more evident than in the **Prayer Room**, where a 24-hour prayer vigil for world peace began in 1985 and has continued unbroken to this day. The vigil is the heartbeat of the temple and will continue until there is no longer a need. Personal prayer requests may be made in the book outside the door.

Kunzang Palyul Choling students maintain a 24-hour prayer vigil for world peace in the Prayer Room.

Outside, the 36-foot-tall **Enlightenment Stupa** is a focal point of the campus. Stupas are one of the oldest forms of sacred architecture, built to avert war, end famine and promote general well-being. Visiting is believed to bring spiritual comfort and inspiration, and walking clockwise around them while reciting prayers or mantras is encouraged.

More stupas are across River Road in the serene, wooded setting of **Peace Park**. Enjoy meditation gardens at the four points of the compass and in the middle of the park, where the 35-foot-tall golden Migyar Dorje Stupa – dedicated to spiritual and physical well-being – is found.

At Peace Park, everyone is welcome; it's considered sacred land that's for the benefit of all. The park is open from dawn to dusk, offering a great place to relax, reflect, picnic and walk your leashed dog. Pets, in fact, have a special place at KPC.

Everyone is invited to share the serene setting of Peace Park.

Tara's Babies Animal Welfare and the **Garuda Aviary** were both founded under the guidance of Jetsunma. Tara's Babies is a dog and cat rescue organization that participates in the no-kill movement, and the Garuda Aviary provides sanctuary for abandoned, abused and neglected large birds such as parrots and macaws.

Next to the temple, the Garuda Aviary – usually open on Saturday afternoons – lends a new understanding about the plight of our unfortunate feathered friends.

Most people purchase large birds for beauty and entertainment, usually with the best of intentions. But the constant screeching and chewing grows old, leading 1.2 million birds to be abandoned annually or to suffer from neglect or abuse. The Garuda Aviary provides a life-long sanctuary, offering food, stimulation and a loving environment. If your timing is right, you'll see the birds in their healing environment.

The **Mani Jewel Gift Store** sells incense, wind chimes, meditation cushions and other items, as well as books on the teachings of Jetsunma and other Buddhist masters. A visit to the shop will give you a chance to bring a little feng shui home with you.

In the DC area, we're pretty good at juggling five balls and a plate in the air at the same time – with one hand tied behind our backs. Most of us are rabid overachievers, and we kind of like it that way. But a day at Kunzang Palyul Choling is a day to enjoy the unexpected. And that peaceful, easy feeling lingers all the way home.

Enjoy the tragic beauty of rescued macaws and parrots at the Garuda Aviary.

Elaine C. Jean

The campus of Kunzang Palyul Choling offers a place for all to relax and reflect.

FYI:

- Sunday Service includes a food ceremony; the public is welcome.
- Visitors should not wear unreasonably revealing clothing.
- Please sign in at the temple before hiking in Peace Park for your safety.
- The gift shop is open daily.
- For additional information, visit www.tara.org.
- Shoes must be removed before entering the Prayer Room and the Teaching Room.

Some wineries offer food pairings, and the chocolates at 8 Chains North
never fail to please.

Elaine C. Jean

Loudoun County, Virginia: Warm up at a winery

Day tripping 101: You don't have to drive for hours to have fun, and you really should talk to strangers whenever the opportunity arises. A little wine can make that happen.

Loudoun County is home to more wineries than any other county in Virginia, and most provide a pleasant way to enjoy the countryside and escape the daily grind for an afternoon. And since each winery reflects the personality, philosophy and taste buds of its owners, there's something for everyone.

This trip is a hop, skip and jump through the vineyards, to some of the warmest, friendliest spots you'll find just outside our nation's capital.

The first stop is **Sunset Hills Vineyard** (38295 Fremont Overlook Lane) in Purcellville, perched on an idyllic 45 acres north of town. Owners Mike and Diane Canney are fond of saying they turn sunshine into wine here, with a total of 154 solar panels running their winery and winemaking operation. The warmth of the sun also fills a 140-year-old barn that houses a drop-dead gorgeous tasting room and features a soaring 35-foot, cathedral-style ceiling.

The Amish-built and carved mahogany bar makes a grand showpiece, not just for its massive presence but for the wines it pours. An inexpensive tasting gives you the opportunity to sample at least six current releases and then buy your favorite by the glass or the bottle. Sunset Hills is known for its fun and floral Viogner, as well as its spicy, jammy Reserve Cabernet Franc.

Live music is featured most weekends – usually of the casual, acoustic variety – and folks mix and mingle freely. It would be very easy to settle in – sipping wine, munching on wood-smoked cheddar and getting to know your fellow oenophiles. But resist the urge, because the next stop involves some serious BBQ.

At the nearby **Hops and Vines** (40602-B Charles Town Pike) in Paeonian Springs, the meat smokes for hours and the sauces are finger lickin' good. All food is made from scratch, and the pulled pork and baked beans pair well with the 2010 LoCo Vino at 8 Chains North. Ask for your grub to go, along with extra napkins.

The folks at our next winery will graciously allow you to bring food in, so long as you don't taunt the other guests with it. For this reason, it's recommend that you stick to one of the relatively discrete BBQ sandwiches, rather than a Flintstone-esque rack of ribs.

8 Chains North ... What's not to love about this spunky, relatively new kid on the block? The winery's tasting room (38593 Daymont Lane) in Waterford is also located in a barn, but this one has been renovated and decorated to look like the comfy, eclectic living room of world traveler J. Peterman. Rich oriental rugs and accents, animal skins and tapestries make the stylish barn warm and inviting.

Owner and winemaker Ben Renshaw has worked in the Virginia wine industry since 1998 and studied with some of the best. As a result, the wines you'll sample at his bar are remarkable refined.

Opt for a tasting and try artisanal chocolates coordinated with the perfect wine. While pairing the food of the gods with the fruit of the vine is nothing new, they take it to a different level when Aztec Heat chocolate meets Furnace Mountain Red Reserve. You'll probably want to stock up on both for the next snow day.

By now you've probably made a few more friends, and you may have even attempted to solve the problems of the world with them. It's amazing how relative strangers will talk about everything imaginable while quaffing the local beverage. You may be tempted to sink into a cushy sofa and join them for the rest of the day, but say your goodbyes, because there's one more winery to visit.

Hunters Run Wine Tasting Barn (40325 Charles Town Pike) in Hamilton is a little bit country, a little bit rock and roll. And more than a little bit Irish. The Emerald Isle meets the Hunt in a rustic-looking barn.

Owner Geri Nolan has learned the art and craft of winemaking under the tutelage of a seasoned winemaker from Cave Ridge Winery. Her tasting line-up includes an elegant Viogner, a smooth Charbourcin and a barrel-aged Port. The latter is inspired by Geri's farther and named Hunters Run Todds.

Riding crops, saddles and the like mingle with shamrocks and Irish sayings in a décor that's fun and friendly. Local talent plays live music on Saturdays. Tables surround a small but mighty wood stove that cranks out the BTUs. Folks laugh together, no matter what the weather.

A day exploring our nearby wine country is all about appreciating a glass of wine with kindred spirits. It's a day best enjoyed with friends – the ones you already know, and the ones you're destined to meet.

FYI:

- This trip is best made on a weekend, when all of the wineries are open.
- Hours are seasonal; consult websites for current information.
- The three featured wineries offer cheese, crackers and snacks for sale.
- Designate a driver or hire a limo for a safe and happy experience.
- Policies about pets, outside food and group tastings vary by winery.

While he played for Baltimore for only five months, Babe presides over
Orioles Park at Camden Yards in perpetuity.

Charm City: The Babe, baseball and beer

If you're in town to see the Orioles play, Charm City is one hometown host that knows how to please. Side trips illustrate the local history of our national pastime, and a stop at Heavy Seas Brewery will give you a chance to toast to the sport's good health.

The **Sports Legends Museum at Camden Yards** (301 W. Camden Street), housed in a beautifully restored train station, is a great place to start. Once the grand terminus and headquarters of the B&O Railroad and now one of just a few surviving metropolitan stations in the United States, the building is a fine historic artifact.

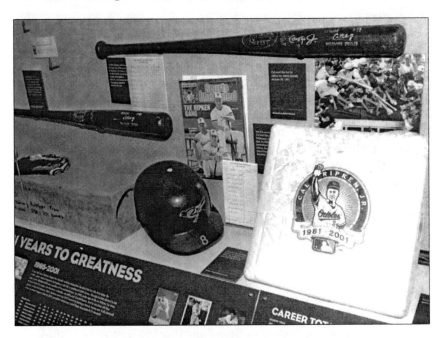

Carl Ripkin Jr. is highlighted in one of the many displays honoring the history, players and fans of the Baltimore Orioles.

The lobby retains its 19th century look and feel. Stroll through a recreated B&O passenger car – complete with moving scenery of the surrounding countryside – and listen to a recording of *Baltimore Sun* reporter Bob Maisel sharing his thoughts on the teams this town loves.

Over a dozen exhibition galleries follow, sharing the history of the Orioles and putting the spotlight on hometown favorites Babe Ruth and Cal Ripkin Jr. The Colts and their pride-and-joy Johnny Unitas are profiled, as well as those relative newcomers, the Baltimore Ravens.

College, minor league baseball and other sports are by no means ignored. The Maryland Athletic Hall of Fame shares the stories of over 200 Maryland athletes in over a dozen different sports.

Follow the 60 baseballs painted on the sidewalk starting in front of the statue of Babe Ruth to visit the birthplace and home of Baltimore's favorite athlete.

The **Babe Ruth Birthplace and Museum** (216 Emory Street) – in what was once the gritty, blue-collar neighborhood of Pigtown – celebrates one of the most revered athletes of all times: George Herman" Babe" Ruth.

Fans flock to the tidy brick row house, deeming it hallowed ground and imagining an eager young boy playing ball out front. But the Bambino's early years were far from idyllic. His parents ran a tavern, sold lightning rods and had little time for their kids.

At the age of seven Babe was sent to St. Mary's, a reform school for ruffians and orphans, where he got a good dose of discipline and learned the industrial arts. He also played quite a bit of baseball.

Babe got his start with the Baltimore Orioles in 1914, but was sold to the Boston Red Sox after a few short months. In 1919 he was again sold – this time to the New York Yankees – and so it's said that the legendary curse of the Bambino began.

The museum displays an extremely rare 1914 Baltimore Orioles rookie card of the man who would become "the Sultan of Swing," as well as a series of molded noses that transformed Stephen Lang into Babe Ruth for a 1991 film. But perhaps the most touching display is of Babe's shirt, bat, mitt and hymnal from St. Mary's.

See the room where Babe Ruth was born in a little house on Emory Street.

If you'd like a little beer with your baseball, hop in the car and take a tour of the **Heavy Seas Brewery** (4615 Hollins Ferry Road). It's only 10 minutes away, and there's plenty of free parking.

Every day is Talk like a Pirate Day at Heavy Seas, although you'll have to sign up ahead of time for one of their popular Saturday tours. Nab a spot with founder Hugh Sisson for a visit that's especially entertaining.

Hugh often starts with a rousing prayer for the successful union of hops, malt, water and yeast. It comes as no surprise that he is, in fact, a failed actor; Hollywood's loss is definitely Baltimore's gain.

This tour appeals to all the senses. You'll walk among a dozen or so towering tanks and their tendrils of hoses, taking in the aroma of fermenting beer, hearing an occasional gurgle, crushing hops in your hands and tasting the roasty toasty barley.

Hugh jumps up on his brewhouse to explain the science of malting and the series of fortunate events that follows. He speaks of starches and molecular bonding, but all you really need to know is that he knows how to make great beer.

Whether you're a hop head or a malt lover, you will appreciate the dedication of the Heavy Seas mission to combine big flavor profiles with a sense of balance and finesse. These aren't just pretty words, they're really doing it.

A tour of the works is inexpensive and includes a souvenir pint glass and five tokens to exchange for tastings. Arrive early or stay late to cash them in and try some of the Heavy Seas fleet of extremely drinkable beers – Small Craft Uber Pils, Peg Leg Imperial Stout, Loose Cannon IPA or whatever other goodness is on tap.

Heavy Seas hosts special events all year long. Their Beer and Bacon Fest in September and Chili and Cheese Fest in November require reservations and sell out quickly.

Argh! See you therrrre!

Hugh Sission leads a lively tour of the works, where you'll learn about the art and science of brewing craft beer.

FYI:

- Plan this trip for a Saturday to enjoy all of its elements.
- The museums are closed on Mondays and major holidays.
- Museum hours are limited from October to March and on game days.
- A combo ticket for admission is reasonably priced.
- Arrive early to nab on-street, metered parking near Camden Station.
- Heavy Seas Brewery is closed on Sundays.
- For additional info, visit www.hsbear.com.

Carpe Weekend's tip:

Tours of the Heavy Seas Brewery are popular and book up weeks in advance. Plan ahead and sign up at www.hsbeer.com as soon as you have a date in mind.

The Garden Court's attractive setting will draw you into the United States Botanic Garden.

United States Botanic Garden: Save it for a rainy day

Rain cascading down the sides of the gigantic greenhouse that is the U.S. Botanic Garden in Washington, DC only enhances its beauty. The humidity and warmth of this place of the earth invites you in on a cold, wet day as if Mother Nature, herself, were standing at the door.

The **Garden Court** of the **US Botanic Garden Conservatory** (100 Maryland Avenue SW) is all decked out with fragrant pots of flowers, as if to extend Mom's welcome and set the stage for what awaits. The heady scent of camellia combines with soothing background music, giving visitors a soothing spot to relax before setting out to explore the varied ecosystems of the world.

Enter the **Jungle** and the humidity level is stepped up a few notches to support abundant palm trees, ferns, bromeliads, prayer plants and philodendron – all plants I've tried but failed to grow at home. Interpretive signage explains the rain cycle of the rain forest, and now I know why I didn't stand a chance.

Wooden walkways and stone bridges are built into the landscape, or, rather, enveloped by it. Steel stairs and a catwalk crawling with vines let you walk among the treetops, and the kid in you may feel a bit like George of the Jungle. Back on the ground, the whimsy continues in a children's garden that's a fantasy of topiary, fern and blossoms.

The transition to **World Desserts** is jarring, with its red rocks and prickly cacti in sharp contrast to the preceding room. But a dry, mineral-scented breeze stirs, and the beauty of the dessert becomes apparent. Dessert flowers that dot the landscape's dusty tones appear to be showing off.

The U.S. Botanic Garden's Conservatory provides an escape from rainy days.

In **Hawaii**, a vignette that includes a waterfall and stone archway in cool, green lusciousness makes real the oft-used marketing slogan Land of Enchantment. At the **Garden Primeval**, a glorious mystery is revealed: Where did all the flowers come from?

The plants in this recreation of the Jurassic Period of the Mesozoic era are living representatives of the vegetation that dominated the planet 150 million years ago. Kids will love the occasional carnivorous plant; letting imaginations run wild is easy when you've stepped back in time and are standing next to a pond that looks like the manifestation of primordial soup.

An exhibit on **Medicinal Plants** showcases the usual suspects – aloe, ginger, lavender, coffee, tea and herbs – as well as witch hazel, goldenseal wild cherry and other homeopathic remedies used to cure everything from bad breath to insomnia.

The **Orchid Room** is a spectacular conclusion. Blooms that range from soft and subdued to loud and happy surround the visitor, set against a background of mossy rocks, deep green leaves and a babbling brook. Blood pressure drops, the spirit soars and suddenly you realize that you haven't felt better in ages.

The outdoor **National Garden** makes a great stroll on a clear day, featuring both native plants of the Mid-Atlantic region and an organic rose garden that honors our national flower. **Historic Bartholdi Park** – created in 1932 – is a local favorite secret garden, with its home landscaping and innovative plant combinations.

The U.S. Botanic Garden is located next to the U.S. Capitol Building and hosts special exhibits, programs and concerts throughout the year.

FYI:

- This trip has year round appeal.
- The US Botanic Garden is open every day, and admission is free.
- Most areas are handicapped accessible, and wheelchairs are available.
- Photography is permitted, and tripod use requires prior authorization.
- Strollers are permitted but may be restricted during peak times.
- The nearest Metro stops are Federal Center SW and Capitol South.
- Metered parking and handicapped designated spaces are available.

Carpe Weekend's tip:

A Junior Botanist Kit is available at the front desk for children ages 9-12.

A cruise on the Skipjack Minnie V provides a quick escape with historical and ecological notes.

Skipjack Minnie V: Sail into history

A cruise aboard the Skipjack Minnie V, departing from Alexandria, Virginia, gives a glimpse of the region's oyster-harvesting past – at once lowering blood pressure and raising awareness for an iconic treasure and its endangered habitat.

The **Potomac Riverboat Company's Minnie V** is one of the hand-built, sloop-rigged oyster boats that enjoyed its heyday on the Chesapeake Bay over a century ago, navigating shallow waters and dredging for what was then one of the most valuable commodities on the East Coast.

The skipjack became the official boat of Maryland in 1985. And the Minnie V – a rare and intact example of the humble-yet-elegant vessel – is a hard worker to this day. Every weekend she transports bi-peds rather than bi-valves on a quest to catch a cool breeze, escape the pressures of life near the nation's capital and learn more about an industry that's all-but-extinct.

The relaxing 90-minute cruise is offered throughout the summer months and continues to set sail from the **Alexandria Marina** in Old Town during weekends until the end of October. A late-afternoon trip up and down the Potomac River in early autumn highlights both the changing sky and the transitional quality of the season.

The Minnie V's experienced captain and crew do all the heavy lifting – hoisting her sail to harness the power of the wind – while as many as 20 passengers sit back and enjoy familiar sights.

It doesn't take much more than a squint to look back in time. Along with all the sun and fun comes a history lesson, with several pointed comments about the health – or lack thereof – of the largest estuary in the United States and its tributaries. These folks clearly love what they do and have a deep and abiding respect for the waters on which they work.

Alexandria's waterfront boardwalk is alive with music, kids and dogs.

One of only 30 skipjacks in existence, the Minnie V began life in 1906 on Maryland's Eastern Shore. Her builder, John B. Vetra of Deale Island, christened the craft in honor of his wife, and the Minnie V spent her first 87 years industriously licking oyster beds and dredging for the much-desired mollusks.

In 1884, when the oyster harvest was at its most bountiful, more than 1,000 skipjacks plied their trade on the Chesapeake Bay to harvest approximately 15 million bushels; in contrast only 43,000 bushels were gathered last year. The steep decline in the oyster harvest is due mainly to disease, over-fishing and water pollution.

Since oysters are Mother Nature's filtration system, our oxygen-poor waters are no longer clear. Run-off from homes, farms and industries nourish large algal blooms that block vital sunlight, and the diminished oyster population just can't keep up on their essential task. While in pre-

Colonial times it took approximately 3.3 days to filter the Bay, the process now takes nearly one year.

Efforts to improve the health of the Bay – beginning with the 1972 Clean Water Act – have fallen short, despite vast scientific understanding of the problem. The Chesapeake Bay Foundation has created a blueprint for protection and restoration, calling upon the six states in the Bay's watershed to address the entire system as a single ecological entity.

The skipjack fleet has been deemed endangered, as well. It's the last class of commercial fishing vessel under the power of sail in the United States and has been included on the National Trust for Historic Preservation's list of America's most endangered historic places.

Occasionally one of the remaining skipjacks may be spotted working the waters around Norfolk and Baltimore. And the Chesapeake Bay Maritime Museum in St. Michael's houses the largest collection of original Chesapeake Bay watercraft in the world, along with exhibits designed to bring the history, culture and ecology of the region to life.

Crew members do all the work – so you don't have to – for a safe and comfortable cruise.

The museum initiated the Skipjack Restoration Project in 2001 and is currently in the process of lovingly restoring the Skipjack Rosie Parks to its former glory, using local wood and boat building techniques. You can check their progress by visiting the museum's Working Boatyard or reading the Chesapeake Bay Boats Blog, found at www.cbmm.org.

The Potomac Riverboat Company's Minnie V was refurbished and rebuilt by Lebourne Smith in 1981 for use as a floating classroom, as well as for private charters and sightseeing. Her graceful cruise along the Potomac River offers a valuable link to Bay's past, one that's fading all too quickly.

If the walls of the **Fish Market** (105 King Street) could talk … They'd tell tales of the sea. The charming antique buildings that now house a lively seafood restaurant and bar were originally used for storing ships' cargo from around the world at a time when Alexandria ranked third – behind New York and Boston – of the busiest ports on the East Coast.

In the century that followed, the facility was called to duty as a hospital for the care of Civil War soldiers and later as a warehouse for the aging and curing of ham, beef and farm products. Here Chirp soda was proudly produced in the early 1900s, and beer was clandestinely brewed during Prohibition.

Now the Fish Market is owned by the Landini family. Its menu includes soups and stews, appetizers, salads, sandwiches, grilled platters, fried fish dishes and piles and piles of big, briny oysters on the half shell. Next door the Anchor Bar offers live entertainment on Saturday nights, along with craft beer on tap and a late-night raw bar menu.

Tuck into the Skipjack Oyster Tower – two dozen premium and one dozen local oysters – with your shipmates. And if you still have room, slide on over to **Pop's Old Fashioned Ice Cream Company** (109 King Street) for a scoop of Bailey's Irish Cream or one of two dozen other homemade flavors usually offered. It's all good!

FYI:

- The Minnie V sails on weekends from mid-May to the end of October.
- A minimum of ten passengers is required for the last cruise of the day.
- Tickets are available online or at the marina.
- Children must be no younger than four and accompanied by an adult.
- Visit www.potomacriverboatco.com for schedule and details, and call ahead to confirm times and availability.

The National Park Service operates a Visitors Center in the Cushwa
Warehouse, open from Wednesday through Sunday.

The C&O Canal: Pedal to the past in Maryland

Williamsport's stretch of the C&O is home to an impressive array of canal architecture, and the nearby village has long enjoyed a tradition of welcoming travelers. Their dedicated bike lane leads directly from trail to town, so cyclists can stop by, relax and recharge at a handful of quaint restaurants and shops.

The Chesapeake & Ohio Canal Historical Park is the 184.5-mile swath of public land that resulted from our nation's attempt to link Georgetown to Pittsburgh via navigable waterway. While the Grand Old Ditch was only used commercially from 1831 to 1924, its towpath has been reborn as a refuge for bikers, hikers and anglers.

Bikers love the uninterrupted hard-packed trail that's akin to a one-lane dirt road with no cars. Most favor hybrid bikes or touring cycles with slightly knobby tires, but just about anything will do except a high-speed racing bike with skinny tires.

Because the trail is built on old railroad and canal beds, it's fairly level with only gentle rises at the lift locks. It's best to don a helmet, since bike laws apply by county and the speed limit is a modest 15 mph. This trail isn't a training ground for the spandex set, so it's a great place for kids and riders of various skill levels.

The **Cushwa Coal and Brick Warehouse** in Williamsport (205 W. Potomac Street) hosts a **Visitor Center** that's currently operated by the National Park Service as a gateway to the park. Here and in the nearby trolley barn, dioramas, displays, photographs and the interpretation of knowledgeable docents bring to life stories of the hundreds of families who devoted their lives to making the great machine run.

The recommended entry point is at **Mile 99.6** and takes the rider past the Cushwa Basin, once the busiest turning basin on the canal because it was used for boats transporting coal inland. The Conococheague Aqueduct is found here, as well.

Along the trip downstream is Western Maryland Railroad's circa 1923 railroad lift bridge, once used to move coal to a nearby power plant. A Bollman truss bridge was built in 1879 and is one of the only bridges of its kind remaining in America.

At **Lock 44** a ranger often operates the gates during weekends. This visual aid helps visitors wrap their brains around a concept that's best described as an elevator for boats. The nearby lock house provides an example of how the lock tender and his family lived.

North of the Visitors Center at **Mile 106.6** is Dam 5. This stone masonry dam provided the water for a hydroelectric power plant on the opposite side of the river. At Mile 108.8 is the shortcut across Prather's Neck known as Four Locks, and what was once a community of homes with a school, post office, dry dock, two warehouses and two stores. Several historic buildings remain in the tiny ghost town.

Lock House 49 is furnished in the style of the 1920s and offers an opportunity to experience canal life by staying the night. Reservations may be made by calling (301) 745-8888 or at www.canalquarters.org.

The historic town of Williamsport offers a variety of shops and restaurants to make your trip more pleasant. Just two blocks from the C&O Canal, **River City Cycles** (16 ½ N. Conococheague Street) is ready to help if you need a tool, accessories or apparel. If you've experienced technical difficulties out on the trail, definitely stop by and see owner Scott Gordon.

This guy knows bikes – he's been riding for 20 years and racing for 17 of them. His is a small full-service shop that sells some of the things you want and everything you need. Scott carries a full line of Giant, Fuji and Kestrel bikes for riders of all ages and skill levels, and he does repair work on all brands.

The **Desert Rose Café** (42 N. Conococheague Street) claims to serve karma by the cup, and they are particularly good to the hungry, tired traveler. A large bike rack outside provides safe haven for your wheels, and the restaurant does the same for your soul.

This is, put simply, a happy place. Rose presides over her kitchen, producing unpretentious, yet high quality food for breakfast, lunch and dinner. Sandwiches are huge and made from your choice of breads, and all salads are served on a bed of organic greens. Smoothies and fancy coffee drinks are the beverages of choice.

The setting is soothing, with comfy chairs and textured wall hangings. This is the place to recharge, grab some healthy grub, meet kindred spirits and see today's Williamsport.

FYI:

- To best enjoy this trip, plan for a spring, summer or fall weekend day.
- The C&O Visitors Center is closed Mondays and Tuesdays in winter.
- To learn more, visit www.williamsportmd.gov/canal.
- River City Cycles is closed on Mondays.
- Desert Rose Café is open seven days per week; hours vary by season.

Flowers can have an other-worldly appearance when viewed through the lens.

Meadowlark Botanical Gardens: A photographer's romp

Driving down Northern Virginia roads that wind past the second largest retail center on the East Coast – along with McMansions, McDonald's and other stuff-of-life in the technovillage known as Tysons Corner – it's difficult to envision the sense of peace a visit to Meadowlark Botanical Gardens will bring. And that's exactly what makes this day trip an unexpected treasure.

Walking trails start at Vienna's **Meadowlark Botanical Gardens Visitors Center** (9750 Meadowlark Gardens Court) and lead to a 95-acre feast for the eyes – a wonderland of ornamental display gardens, native plant collections, lakes, gazebos and artistic sculptures. Your camera will grant access to the world-within-a-world, revealing the fat, fuzzy bodies of bumblebees as well as the silvery green wool of the lamb's ear plant.

Any day is a great day to appreciate colorful gardens and intoxicating scents. But **Meadowlark's Photographers' Field Day**, offered twice a year, gives a special look – with extended hours and several classes aimed at the beginner through the expert shutterbug.

During a recent event a professional photographer gathered advanced students at the crack of dawn and led them on a sunrise macro tour, sharing tips for capturing the finer detail of flowers and insects. The crew trekked along, discussing the art of the up-close-and-personal and carting around equipment that was probably worth more than my house.

Later that day, the same guide had equal enthusiasm instructing beginners wielding point-and-shoot cameras, sharing the basics of using more humble equipment to take great pictures.

This gazebo offers a quiet spot to reflect on the day and enjoy Meadowlark.

Local photographers are fond of visiting the gardens throughout the seasons, so they especially appreciate this rare opportunity to capture the magic hour at Meadowlark – that fleeting time when lighting is optimal and only the clicking of shutters and the chirping of birds dares disturb the silence.

For those who prefer to view the world with the naked eye and not through a lens, there's still plenty to see without getting up at the crack of dawn, having special equipment or making reservations.

The gardens are open every day by mid-morning – except on major holidays – and closing time varies by month. Several collections are assembled by theme and purpose – the **Herbal Potpourri Garden, Butterfly Garden, Pollenators Garden** and **Perennial Color Border**. Others display plants that are native to the Potomac River Valley – wild hydrangea, tulip poplar and azalea.

Trails loop through the park, and every once in a while you'll stumble upon a thoughtfully displayed sculpture – a massive pine cone under a mighty conifer tree, or a rusty rhino in the rough. The pieces enjoy their outdoor gallery while on a rotational program, and most are for sale.

Two lakes serve as centerpieces for the park: **Lake Lina** with its boardwalk and wetlands bog garden, and **Lake Caroline** with a gazebo and flowering cherries, irises, peonies and daylilies. Marshy areas are dotted with water lilies and cat o' nine tails, and fish and turtles make them home.

Kids love to feed the fish with food that's available in the Visitors Center for a small fee. Children also love the huge sand box near the water, and a **Garden Tea House** that's right out of a fairy tale.

New to Meadowlark is the 4.7 acre **Korean Bell Garden**, featuring a traditional Korean pavilion with a cast iron bell that was handcrafted in Korea using a centuries-old technique. This is the first Korean Bell Garden in North America, and it was funded by the Korean American Cultural Committee with financial support from the Republic of Korea.

A rustic, **18th century log cabin** is found at a clearing in the woods, and it's all that remains of the home of Gardiner Means and Caroline Ware. The couple – he an economics professor and she an author, educator and social historian – met at Harvard University and came to the Washington area to help FDR craft the New Deal in 1935.

The bell in the Korean Bell Garden was made with a process used since 700 AD.

They lived in a farmhouse that once enveloped the one-room log cabin, and when Means and Ware discovered the humble homestead they exposed its logs to enhance their living room. Here they entertained friends, who helped them harvest wheat, pick apples and make cider in exchange for dinner and lively conversation.

Gardiner Means and Caroline Ware donated 50 acres of their land to the Northern Virginia Regional Park Authority in 1980, and in 1990 – three years after Means passed away – Ware deeded them the house and an additional 23 acres. She died shortly thereafter, but the legacy of this forward-thinking couple lives on.

Meadowlark Botanical Gardens is a property of the NVRPA. Beauty, conservation, education and discovery flourish here, and Gardiner Means and Caroline Ware would surely be pleased.

Idyllic scenes greet visitors at every turn.

The Visitors Center offers maps, information and a blazing fire in winter.

FYI:

- Visit www.nvrpa.org for details about Photographers' Field Day.
- Admission is inexpensive.
- Paved trails are stroller and wheelchair friendly.
- Meadowlark offers classes on a variety of topics.
- Picnic tables are near the parking lot; food is not allowed in the park.
- Dogs are not allowed inside Meadowlark, but they are welcome on the perimeter trail.

The Last Portrait of Abraham Lincoln from Life, by Alexander Gardner,
was taken on February 5, 1865.
Courtesy of Library of Congress, Prints and Photographs Division

4. TIME TRAVEL MADE EASY

Lincoln's Cottage: Abe Lincoln, up close and personal

Hidden in plain sight on the grounds of the Armed Forces Retirement Home in Washington, DC, Lincoln's Cottage affords the visitor a rare opportunity to connect with the humble-yet-complex man who was our 16th president.

Abraham Lincoln used the 34-room Gothic Revival house on the outskirts of the nation's capital as a retreat – his Camp David – during the summers of 1862, 1863 and 1864, spending a combined one-quarter of his presidency here. At **Lincoln's Cottage** (300 Randolph Street NW) he hoped to escape the heat of the summer, the pressure of the presidency and the stress of the ongoing Civil War.

The president's three-mile daily commute back to the White House took about 40 minutes on horseback or by carriage, about the same as it might today with traffic being what it is. Along the roadside, Lincoln often stopped to talk with wounded soldiers who had just returned from the front. He strived to connect with ordinary people, and the insight he gained from this rapport helped him make decisions in his role as the Commander in Chief.

He felt so at home at the cottage that he referred to his office in the White House as the shop. And while the summer home did provide relief from the daily grind, it didn't prove to be much of an escape from the war. Union camps dotted the grounds, and our first National Cemetery was in plain view of the house – a constant reminder of mounting casualties.

Lincoln was remarkably accessible to the public, and a steady stream of visitors made the trek to see him in the evenings. He received callers in the drawing room, where he willingly chatted with those who casually stopped by.

President Lincoln was most comfortable at his summer cottage.
Courtesy of Library of Congress, Prints and Photographs Division

Today a docent-led tour brings you to the same room, where you'll hear the words of a late-night visitor who arrived unannounced to find the president sporting bedroom slippers and ruffled hair, sharing stories of his modest upbringing.

Abraham Lincoln comes into focus in this place that gave him great comfort – no longer the larger-than-life character of our history books.

Refreshingly down-to-earth and introspective, this man was relatively unspoiled by the trappings of his office.

Unlike many historic sites associated with our past presidents, Lincoln's Cottage is not about furniture and china, or pomp and circumstance. It's about a man who rose to greatness while remaining grounded. It's about a man who loved his country so much that he worked tirelessly to put it back together again, with little regard for personal expense.

In this house Lincoln mourned his young son, and in its library he enjoyed the books of the times. Here he plotted Union war strategy and drafted the Emancipation Proclamation. The last day he visited the cottage was the day before his assassination.

Lincoln's Cottage opened to the public in 2008, after an extensive $15 million restoration project by the National Trust for Historic Preservation. The cottage may only be seen by guided tour, during which visitors walk in the footsteps of Abraham Lincoln and explore the major issues of his presidency – war, freedom and democracy.

Groups are small, and reservations – which are highly recommended – may be made at www.lincolnscottage.org. Tickets for the one-hour tour include admission to the **Robert H. Smith Visitors Center**.

Plan to arrive 15 minutes early to check in at the Visitors Center, and return after the tour to explore displays that give insight on Lincoln's life and times.

Several museum exhibits provide insight on Lincoln's self-deprecating sense of humor – revealed by a display on the 1858 debate with Stephen Douglas. When Douglas accused Lincoln of being two-faced, Lincoln quipped, "I leave it to you, my audience: If I were two-faced, would I be wearing this one?"

A life-size bronze sculpture of our 16th president and his horse, on the grounds outside the cottage, recalls Lincoln's daily commute and further points to the ordinary life of this extraordinary man.

What would Lincoln eat? **Hank's Oyster Bar** at 1624 Q Street NW, a
Dupont Circle favorite, is the ideal spot to enjoy one of Lincoln's
favorite foods after touring his historic summer retreat.

In the mid-1800s oysters were well-established fare in taverns up and
down the East Coast, and so the munchable mollusk migrated westward.
Oyster wagons that were the 19th century equivalent of present-day UPS
trucks rushed briny cargo to big cities, and oyster saloons became
popular meeting places for politicians and public servants.

One country lawyer in Illinois was no exception.

That Abraham Lincoln so embraced this humble pub grub spoke to the
unpretentious nature of the man. He was said to have personally shoveled
out fried oysters to the public as part of his campaign strategy in 1864.

Hank's Oyster Bar serves up oysters – and other seafood – in a down-to-
earth yet stylish setting that's a quick detour off 17th Street on your way
home from Lincoln's Cottage.

Hank's Oyster Bar in Dupont Circle offers seafood and snacks that Lincoln
would approve.

Small plates – oysters and clams on the half-shell, jumbo shrimp cocktail and sake oyster shooters, as well as tender morsels of fried oysters, shrimp and calamari – make satisfying snacks. And large plates such as lobster rolls, seared scallops and fried oysters, make even this New Englander smile.

FYI:

- Parking at Lincoln's Cottage is abundant and free.
- Prepare to show photo ID as you pass the guard shack.
- Tickets are reasonable and may be purchased online and at the door.
- Same-day ticket purchases are subject to availability.
- No strollers or photography are allowed inside the buildings.
- Lincoln's Cottage is open daily except on major holidays.

Carpe Weekend's tip:

Parking near Hank's Oyster Bar is limited, but patience pays off. Ride around the block a couple of times, as cars come and go often and on-street parking can be nabbed in the middle of a weekend afternoon in a matter of minutes. Hank's is worth the effort.

In *Native of Virginia*, Melchers captured a local woman on his canvas.

Home and Studio of Gari Melchers: A lasting impression

Just across the Rappahannock River and outside Fredericksburg,
Virginia, Gari Melchers Home and Studio at Belmont is a time capsule
dedicated to the life of an artist who once enjoyed international acclaim.
A visit will properly acquaint you with his multi-faceted talent, and
surely endear him to you.

Elegant-yet-cozy, **The Home and Studio of Gari Melchers** (224
Washington Street) is filled with personal knick knacks and an eclectic
mix of furnishings, revealing much about Gari Melchers (1860-1932)
and exuding a warmth not typically associated with his period. The
studio tells even more about the talented American impressionist who
explored several distinct styles throughout his career.

Not familiar with the work of Gari Melchers? That makes this day trip
feel a bit like a gift, a fitting analogy since his widow, Corinne, deeded
the estate to the Commonwealth of Virginia in 1942 as a lasting tribute to
her husband.

With a personal mantra of "true and clear," the artist's great talent was in
his honest characterization of the everyday people around him. Melchers
celebrated local villagers caught in routine moments, both in the Dutch
seaside community where he once resided and here, at Belmont.

He also painted the rich and famous, people with the names of
Vanderbilt, Mellon and Roosevelt. His work has timeless appeal for its
depiction of a slice-of-life; Melchers went about the business of
capturing real people on his canvas – whether famous or not – unadorned
and unplugged.

The best way to start the day is with the brief biographical video shown
in the **Visitors Center**, where tickets may be purchased and a wealth of

information is given away. Next, a tour of the couple's gracious home brings their lives into focus.

Gari and Corinne Melchers created a comfortable retreat at Belmont.

As a docent leads you through each room, you'll get to know Gari and Corinne Melchers through stories about their courtship, daily routines, marriage and partnership. And you'll feel their presence through abundant signs of life – keys, books, reading glasses, a shaving kit and even Dutch clogs from Gari's early days in Holland. It's as if our hosts have just stepped out to visit the local pub.

Their personal art collection fills the walls, and anecdotes about these special paintings have a certain entertainment value. You quickly get the idea that Gari and Corinne Melchers were madly in love with each other, and that they were fun, likeable people.

That's not to say that Gari Melchers wasn't serious about his work. Those who knew him well described him as a man who, quite simply, lived to paint.

The artist's devotion is evidenced by a visit to the nearby studio building, which Melchers designed in 1924 to incorporate a dramatic window granting him that one essential ingredient: Northern light.

Stepping into the studio allows you to enter his creative world, brought to life with Melchers' original tools – worn and aged tubes of paint, varnish, pastels and brushes, as well as numerous paintings by the artist and his colleagues.

Of note is an unfinished painting, *From the Porch*, with a small practice piece next to it. The work was probably in progress at the time of the artist's death in 1932.

The studio and its two lower galleries showcase the span of Melchers' career – from his beginning as a realistic painter, through the Dutch years, and to his celebrated period as an American impressionist.

Many of the paintings from his time at Belmont –when he walked the streets of Falmouth in white coveralls looking for subjects to paint – are on display. It is these paintings that made him famous in the art circles of both New York City and San Francisco.

The artist designed his creative space to exude an old-world flavor.

Be sure to explore the grounds of the 27-acre retreat, where outbuildings include a spring house, smoke house, cow barn and stable. Trails at Belmont lead through groomed gardens and along woodland walks, and a free map is available at the Visitors Center. Although the trip to the river takes just 20 minutes, the terrain is uneven so proper footwear is recommended.

Finally, linger in the colorful, restored gardens on stone pathways that are lined with boxwood shrubs and trimmed with rose-covered arbors – the perfect place to ponder the life of an artist who might almost be forgotten yet still has the power to delight.

Would Gari Melchers mind that his work no longer receives the recognition that it once did? Possibly not. He woke up every day to witness the pastoral beauty of this retreat. He found and married the love of his life. And every single day, he got to do what he loved most of all.

As Melchers once explained, "Nothing matters in the world to the painter, but a good picture."

FYI:

- Tickets are reasonable for adults and free for students 18 and under.
- Picnic tables are scattered throughout the grounds.
- The museum is administered by the University of Mary Washington.
- Open daily except on Wednesdays and major holidays.
- To enhance your tour, watch *True and Clear* before visiting at www.umw.edu/gari_melchers.

Amy's Café (103 W. Cambridge Street) is housed in a cozy 200-year-old brick building in the historic Falmouth Bottom neighborhood. This structure and many of the others in the small village have changed little since Gari and Corrine Melchers lived at Belmont, and photos of their old 'hood line the walls.

Amy's serves old-fashioned breakfasts, soups, salads, appetizers and dinners, plus a decent array of beer and wine; you'll hear live acoustic music here on Saturday afternoons.

Stop by for some loaded nachos, a couple of beers and a history lesson. Amy's staff is proud to tell customers that the building is constructed mostly of ballast bricks from cargo ships, and that it has served as a tavern, a cotton warehouse and a general store.

With all those previous lives, you've got to wonder if the place is haunted. Ask to see compelling photographic evidence of paranormal activity, and visit on a dark and stormy night to decide for yourself.

Amy's Café is a great spot to grab a bite and meet some of the locals.

Clara Barton was the celebrity-in-residence at Glen Echo Park from 1897 to 1912.
Courtesy of Library of Congress, Prints and Photographs Division

Glen Echo Park: Home to the Angel of the Battlefield

Clara Barton dedicated her life to the mending of the body in times of conflict and natural disaster. It makes perfect kharmic sense that she lived her final years at Glen Echo Park in Maryland, a place dedicated to the nurturing of the mind and spirit.

Glen Echo Park (7300 MacArthur Boulevard) was established in 1888 when two brothers with a newfangled design for a better egg beater used fame and fortune to stir up the local real estate market. Edwin and Edward Baltzey purchased 516 acres along the Potomac River with the lofty goal of developing a neighborhood that was much more than a place to live, offering an opportunity for residents to learn and grow right in their own backyards.

The brothers Baltzey envisioned that their location would include a nationally recognized Chautauqua center, hosting the family-friendly summer camps that were made popular by Methodists in New York. Chautauquas offered the culture of the city – speakers, musicians, entertainers and preachers – in a comfortable rural setting.

By the late 19th century the movement was in full swing, and Glen Echo was chosen as the location of the 53rd Chautauqua Assembly in 1891. In order to accommodate the park's summer visitors the Baltzeys went big on their design, building a 6,000-seat amphitheater perched over Minnehaha Creek with a speaker system fueled by water power. They even attracted Clara Barton, the founder of the American Red Cross, to live in their community. The brothers appeared to be unstoppable.

Despite a successful launch, the second year was problematic due to poor weather conditions and an economic downturn. The Chautauqua soon ended, and the park evolved to include encampments, vaudeville acts and operas. In 1899 amusement rides arrived on the scene.

By 1903 Glen Echo had become a destination for trolley riders – providing a full day of entertainment for the price of a train ride – and by 1911, the park had been enhanced to include a dance pavilion, human roulette wheel and more. Over the years, Glen Echo became known as a state-of-the-art venue with a swimming pool to cool 3,000 bathers.

The 7,500-square-foot **Spanish Ballroom** was a centerpiece, offering big bands of the era. The park's popularity peaked in the 1940s, and attendance dropped off severely from 1944-1950. Glen Echo closed in 1968 amid social unrest over civil rights; the harsh reality was that the park had failed to become integrated in a graceful manner.

The National Park Service took over Glen Echo in 1970, and a renaissance began that would transform it into a cultural center. Today a partnership between the National Park Service, Montgomery County and the Town of Glen Echo manages its multi-faceted activities.

The park is now best known for its social dances, ranging from American Swing to Contra and Square Dance and held in the restored ballroom on Thursdays, Fridays, Saturdays and Sundays. They're open to the public, and the cost of admission includes a free lesson.

Resident artists specializing in pottery, calligraphy, glasswork, photography and music hold exhibitions, studio hours and classes for children and adults, and festivals and special events are offered several times each year.

Visitors can also explore nature, ride the **1921 Dentzel Carousel**, take in a puppet show, enjoy the thriving artist community, romp in the playground and have a picnic at Glen Echo Park. The vision of the Baltzey brothers has been realized after all, and Glen Echo has come full circle.

A tour of the nearby **Clara Barton National Historic Site** reveals much about the founder of the American Red Cross. In this 38-room home, Barton lived, worked, stored supplies and housed volunteers, often blurring the line between personal life and vocation to the point of nonexistence.

Best known as the Angel of the Battlefield, Barton took care of wounded soldiers from both sides of the Mason-Dixon Line and corresponded with their families, enlisting them to send supplies to their loved ones.

When the Civil War ended she launched a national campaign to identify missing soldiers, which took a significant toll on her spirit. She was ordered to take a trip to Europe by her doctor, but there's no rest for the weary, as we all know.

Barton joined the relief effort to aid soldiers of the war between France and Prussia, where she witnessed the Red Cross in action. When she returned to America, her life had a renewed purpose, and she founded the American Red Cross to provide aid for the victims of natural disaster.

In 1891, the Baltzeys lured Barton to Glen Echo with the promise of free labor for the construction of her residence and a beautiful knoll of land on which to build it. Both creative and frugal, Barton designed a stunning home that exuded warmth and comfort yet remained practical, with hidden nooks and crannies in which to stow bandages and other tools of the healing trade.

The house is restored to give a glimpse of her life there until her death at the age of 90 in 1912. A tour gives visitors a unique opportunity to get to know an outstanding American humanitarian who, with no formal nursing background, devoted her life to healing the wounded.

FYI:

- Weekend tours of Glen Echo Park are free.
- Inexpensive carousel rides are offered from May – September.
- Visit www.glenechopark.org for hours of operation and fees.
- Tours of Clara Barton's home are free and meet on the porch.
- Parking is abundant and free; the park is closed on major holidays.
- For details about the Clara Barton National Historic Site visit www.nps.gov/clba.

Trails within Mason Neck State Park offer scenic views of the local marshes.

Gunston Hall: Where eagles soar

Founding Father George Mason championed personal rights and individual liberties. Appropriately, the Virginia home of the author of the Bill of Rights now shares a peninsula with 6,000 acres dedicated to the protection of the bald eagle – our symbol of strength and freedom.

Mason Neck is not always the first place that comes to mind when looking for a great escape. That's puzzling because two-thirds of its land is preserved by regional, state and federal authorities, making it the oasis that's just around the corner from Washington, DC.

The peninsula is tucked in southeastern Fairfax County and surrounded on three sides by water – the Potomac River, Gunston Cove and Belmont and Pohick Bays. History swirls around this swath of land, as well.

Mason Neck takes its name from a family who made quite an impact on the colony of Virginia. Georges all, they were politicians, landowners and farmers.

Our Founding Father was fourth in line, a private man who was both a successful tobacco planter and reluctant politician. By 1755 he was living on what was then known as Doegs' Neck, and he began construction on Gunston Hall, named for his ancestral home in England.

Today **Gunston Hall**, (10709 Gunston Road), is open to the public. Ironically, George Mason's accomplishments are better known in Europe than in the United States, and a visit to his home is a must for lovers of liberty and students of democracy. A guided tour affords the opportunity to get to know a true American patriot who has become a bit of a mystery.

To begin the day, watch a brief orientation film about Mason's life in the **Visitors Center**, and learn about his significant contributions as author of the Virginia Declaration of Rights. Then gather on the front porch of the mansion to meet up with a docent.

Gunston Hall is a must-see for lovers of liberty and students of democracy.

While Mason designed the Georgian-style home and was involved with its construction, he did have the assistance of a talented team – comprised of carpenter-joiner William Buckland and carver William Bernard Sears. And it should be noted that enslaved African Americans made up the majority of the workforce of craftsman who contributed to the project.

The wealth of the man who owned this manor is evidenced by its elaborately carved woodwork and exquisite 18th century furniture. Since many of the mansion's furnishings were used by the Mason family during their time here, the visitor gets an accurate peek at how they lived.

A tour of the upstairs is self-guided. Be sure to walk through the yard and visit the garden, kitchen yard, slave quarter site, schoolhouse, burial ground and nature trail to the river, as well. A museum shop, interpretive exhibits and restrooms are found in the Visitors Center, and a picnic area is nearby.

George Mason served on the building committee for **Pohick Church** (9301 Richmond Road), along with George Washington. Our first president was a surveyor, so he found the perfect spot for the church – halfway between Gunston Hall and Mount Vernon. Even that did not ensure a friendship between the two great men, who held conflicting views during the writing of the Constitution.

A guide for a recommended walking tour is available inside the church, so you can literally walk in the footsteps of our Founding Fathers. And you can attend services here on Sundays to take in the surroundings from where both Washington and Mason once worshipped. Handcrafted needlepoint kneelers and seat covers depict their respective homes and illustrate the talents of the more recent Pohick Church community.

George Mason served on the building committee for Pohick Church.

Found on High Point Road, **Elizabeth Hartwell Mason Neck National Wildlife Refuge** opened in 1969 as the first national wildlife refuge established for the nesting, feeding and roosting of the bald eagle. Such measures have brought the bird back from the brink of extinction, sharing its 2,227-acre park with migrating ducks, raptors and songbirds.

Several trails bring the day hiker into this limited-access sanctuary, and the most accessible is the **Great Marsh Trail** on Gunston Road. After a paved, level hike of nearly one mile, you'll be rewarded with a platform offering a sweeping view of one of the largest freshwater marshes on the river.

Another platform may be reached from the three-mile-long **Woodmarsh Trail**, a circuit hike with parking on High Point Road. This trail is composed of gravel and compacted dirt, and it's subject to becoming muddy following rainstorms. Proper footwear is recommended.

The **High Point Trail** is also three miles long and paved for use by both hikers and bikers. The trail begins in the Woodmarsh Trail parking lot and leads through the wildlife refuge and over to Mason Neck State Park.

Mason Neck State Park offers a peaceful retreat with a view.

Right next door, **Mason Neck State Park** shares the mission of protecting the bald eagle. A fantastic family destination, it offers several easy hiking trails and a couple of moderate ones, as well as a playground, picnic area, restrooms and a canoe and kayak launch.

Canoe and kayak rentals are available at the **Visitors Center** from April through October, and you can book guided expeditions along Belmont Bay and Kane's Creek. Paddle through the natural habitat of majestic birds and busy beavers on morning, afternoon or evening trips, and see George Mason's stomping ground from a different vantage point. Twilight trips are offered to paddlers over the age of 18 on Friday evenings before or during a full moon. Reservations are required.

FYI:

- Gunston Hall is open daily and closed on major holidays.
- Tours are offered on the half-hour.
- Admission is reasonable, with discounts for seniors and children.
- Pohick Church is open daily; admission is free.
- Admission to Mason Neck State Park is inexpensive.
- Admission to Elizabeth Hartwell Mason Neck National Wildlife Refuge is free.

The George Washington Masonic Memorial offers a bird's eye view of
Old Town Alexandria and beyond.

George Washington's Alexandria: Party like it's 1799

The cobblestone streets of Alexandria, Virginia were once George Washington's stomping ground. Today Old Town is a quaint destination that's a popular choice for day trippers and vacationers alike. Learn more about the life of our first president when he went off the plantation.

Walk in Washington's footsteps, stop in at some of the places he loved, and tour the magnificent memorial that was built in his honor by a grateful brotherhood of Freemasons. This is a rare opportunity to look inside an organization that has traditionally been cloaked in secrecy, and to understand the reverence it holds for Brother Washington.

Whether you believe the Freemasons are a benign organization that's akin to the Kiwanis or an ancient order hell-bent on world domination, you'll enjoy a rare peek behind the curtain at the **George Washington Masonic Memorial** (101 Callahan Drive) in Alexandria.

On Washington's Birthday in 1910, Freemasons from around the country discussed the idea of building a memorial to the man who epitomized their vision of virtue and sacrifices made during a lifetime of public service. Ground was broken in 1922 and the project was completed 10 years later, entirely with private funds collected by the Masons.

The resulting memorial is spectacular. Inspired by the Lighthouse of Alexandria in Egypt, it honors George Washington as a guiding light for both our country and his fraternal organization. Architecture combines Greek and Roman influences in a structure made largely of, not surprisingly, stone. Exhibits show Washington in the context of a Freemason, as well as in his leadership role as Charter Master of Alexandria-Washington Masonic Lodge #22.

Visitors enter on the main level and can buy tickets for entry to the first two floors; a small upcharge gains a guided tour with access to the tower and observatory – worth every penny. It's led by a Freemason who will answer your questions – at least most of them – and bring you up into the tower to see the **George Washington Museum** and several other rooms that are sponsored by Masonic chapters.

The ride in the lush, wood-paneled elevator – with the dozen or so people on the tour – is quick and cozy, and the anticipation is palpable. If you hit it lucky, your trip will be further enhanced by someone who either knows his Dan Brown or claims to be a distant relative of Washington's.

The stunning museum on the fourth floor enlightens visitors about the many roles Washington held – soldier, farmer, president, and, at his core, Freemason. Artifacts include his field trunk from the Revolutionary War, tools from the cornerstone ceremony at the US Capitol Building, strands of his hair and a transcript of his will from the local newspaper.

Ascending the tower you'll visit rooms that feel more like chambers, the first of which is sponsored by the **Royal Arch Chapter**. Borrowing heavily from Egyptian and Hebrew culture, décor of biblical inspiration enhances the walls. A beautiful reproduction of the Ark of the Covenant takes center stage. Think: Indiana Jones.

The **Knights Templar** room is of Medieval French Gothic design and was dedicated in 1957 by Vice-President Richard Nixon. It features four enormous stained glass windows – the most significant of which depicts the three degrees of Freemasonry – as well as two suits of armor and the sword of a Crusader. Legend and lore surround the original Knights Templar, and this room captures the mystique.

Tucked away on the ninth floor is a room sponsored by the **Tall Cedars of Lebanon**. It's a breathtaking reconstruction of the temple of King Solomon and the items in it – including his throne, large copper bowl, oil lamp holders and a tree of life. This chapter is best known for its fundraising efforts in the fight against Muscular Dystrophy.

The ninth floor also grants access to the **observation deck**, which circles the top of the tower and boasts a 360-degree view of the Metro area – a full 400 feet above sea level. The US Capitol, Washington Monument, National Harbor and points of interest in Maryland and Virginia are easily spotted, and the town of Alexandria is laid out directly below like a model railroad village.

Back on the main level a colossal bronze statue of Washington in full Masonic regalia – all 17 feet and seven tons of him – graces the entry hall, and murals on each side richly depict important events in his life as a Mason.

Of special note in the gallery behind the gift shop is the chamber clock that marks the time of George Washington's death – 10:20 – on the evening of December 14, 1799. Also included in the room is a chair from Washington's library, in which every Grand Master in Virginia has his official photo taken.

The lower level houses a gallery dedicated to the Shriners, that fun-loving and benevolent group famous for its participation in parades and contributions to children's hospitals. An extensive exhibit provides a crash course on Freemasonry and illustrates how prominent Americans – George Washington, Ben Franklin, Andrew Jackson and Harry Truman – improved themselves as they boosted their communities.

FYI:

- Parking is free at the George Washington Masonic Memorial.
- A small admission fee is charged.
- Proper attire is required.
- The building is handicapped-accessible from the parking lot.
- Strollers, backpacks and baby carriages are prohibited.

After you've met George Washington, the Freemason, consider exploring his stomping ground to learn more about the Father of Our Country as a man about town. The past is woven with the present in Alexandria, making for one stylishly entertaining history lesson.

Drive to the **Ramsay House Visitors Center** (221 King Street) and find on-street parking nearby. Then go inside and ask to become an **Honorary Citizen for the Day**, receiving a parking certificate for your car so you won't have to feed the meter.

This building was once the home of William Ramsay, the first mayor of Alexandria, and it offers a good starting point with plenty of free information, maps and brochures.

Pick up a **restaurant book** containing hundreds of dollars worth of discounts – it's free – and buy **Alexandria's Key to the City** – it's inexpensive and holds coupons for admission to many of the town's attractions, as well as discounts for restaurants and shops.

The **Carlyle House Historic Park** (121 N. Fairfax Street) is the next stop. As a prosperous and influential founder of this city, John Carlyle hosted George and Martha on numerous occasions in his elegant home. It has been beautifully restored to show how Carlyle lived and entertained, giving us a slice of aristocratic life.

Standing in the middle of rooms that George Washington did – and not behind a Plexiglas barrier – helps visitors feel especially connected to the past. Don't expect to see any ghosts, though. A dead cat has been entombed behind one of the walls to ward off paranormal activity.

The Carlyle House is a must-see, and an hour-long tour is reasonably priced (free with a coupon if you purchased the Key to the City). Note that once a year in mid-February, visitors can meet costumed interpreters during the George Washington Comes to Dinner event.

The **Stabler-Leadbetter Apothecary Shop** (105-107 S. Fairfax Street) is now a museum, but from 1792-1933 it was a family-owned pharmacy that cured whatever ailed local residents. Prominent customers included Nelly Custis, Robert E. Lee and Martha Washington, whose request for caster oil is proudly displayed in one of the exhibits.

Visible among the rows of medicine and elixirs are containers for opium and cannabis, as well as lavender for depression and powdered pumpkin seed for tapeworm. Dragonsblood and snakeroot might make you think you've wandered into Diagon Alley, but these are merely colorful names for products in the former company's line of paints and varnishes.

Jars and bottles line the walls, and work benches are outfitted with the tools of the trade; it appears the pharmacist has just stepped out for a coffee break. This museum is unusual in that it was one of the oldest continuously functioning pharmacies in the country when it closed in the 1930s, and the building was sold with all of its items intact. A tour of this time capsule is free with a coupon from the Key to the City.

Gadsby's Tavern (138 N. Royal Street) consists of two buildings – a tavern and an inn – and George Washington really did sleep here.

Gadsby's was the center of social, political and business life in 18th century Alexandria. For two consecutive years, George and Martha attended the annual Birthnight Ball held in his honor at the tavern.

Visitors can tour the historic rooms and dine in the fine restaurant, which serves Washington's favorite meal –glazed breast of duck with scalloped potatoes – and other colonial favorites. Tours are free with a coupon from the Key to the City.

While you can't enter **George Washington's Townhouse** (508 Cameron Street), you can stroll by this reproduction of his in-town dwelling and ponder what went on inside. Washington kept a modest residence in Alexandria for when bad weather struck or business engagements kept him from making the trek back to Mount Vernon.

The Washingtons worshipped at **Old Christ Church** (118 N. Washington Street), an English-style country church. Tours are free and available upon request when a docent is available. The grounds are picturesque, and the graveyard dates back to the 1700s.

The town of Alexandria loves its most famous citizen just as much as it loves to party. Events and special promotions are planned throughout the month of February; for details visit www.washingtonbirthday.net/events.

Carpe Weekend's tip:

Many of the historic attractions in Old Town Alexandria close at 4 p.m. during the winter months. If you go off-season, start the day early to fit in as much fun as you can, and consider an overnight stay.

The Hugh Mercer Apothecary Shop is a little shop of horrors. Where
else can you meet a live leech?

Fredericksburg: Washington's other stomping ground

Fredericksburg, Virginia offers enough historic sites to make your wig spin; the George-Washington-themed attractions alone could fill a long day or an entire weekend. This trip is best suited to a Saturday, when the museums open early and you're more likely to stay in town a little later.

The **Fredericksburg Visitors Center** (706 Caroline Street) is the best place to get started. The doors open at 9 a.m. on Saturdays, and the center offers maps, brochures, discount admission tickets and dining recommendations. Think of these folks as your local travel agents.

A **Timeless Ticket** may be purchased here, granting access to nine area attractions for a savings of 40 percent. If you plan to do everything I did, it makes good sense to pick one up. Any portion of the ticket that doesn't get used initially can be redeemed on another day, so you can't lose.

A 14-minute audiovisual presentation sets the stage for what you will see, and a 75-minute trolley tour – departing from the center for a small fee – will fill in any gaps. You'll get your lay of this land that George Washington once called home, so you can start exploring on your own.

There are a few must-sees and at the top of the list is the **Hugh Mercer Apothecary Shop and Physick Garden** (1020 Caroline Street).

Tours of this circa 1760 little shop of horrors, once frequented by Mary Washington, are given by costumed re-enactors and feature cures for whatever ails you. Tools of the trade – a tooth extractor, a pocket lancet and live leeches – are brandished as the guide describes their uses. My advice? When the doctor's apprentice asks you how you're feeling today, answer, "Just fine, thanks!"

The building that houses the **Rising Sun Tavern** (1304 Caroline Street) was built by Charles Washington at about the same time, and it was originally the residence of the brother of our first president. It was later converted to a tavern, and today bar wenches and indentured servants show you around what was once the bustling port's finest dining and lodging establishment.

The tap room features a reconstructed bar cage and dining area, complete with pewter tankards and faux food. The tour is lively and informative, enlightening participants on the origin of idioms, "Mind your Ps and Qs," "Drink like a fish" and "Bottoms up."

Historic Kenmore (1201 Washington Street) was built in 1775 as the home of George Washington's sister, Betty and her husband, Fielding Lewis. You'll step through an entryway in an ivy-covered wall to gain access to Kenmore's Visitors Center, where dioramas of the Fredericksburg of old bring the past to life.

George Washington's sister Betty and her husband lived at Historic Kenmore.

This Georgian in-town mansion boasts elaborate plasterwork from Colonial America – most of which is original and intact. The dining room at Kenmore is one of the most beautiful rooms in America. Tours of the mansion give insight about the lives of these famous members of the gentry class, as well as the process of creating their homes. Of particular interest is a touching story about the plasterwork done by a young man who may have been destined for his role in history.

The Mary Washington House (1200 Charles Street) was purchased by George for his 64-year-old mother in 1772, so she could live in town and near her daughter Betty at Kenmore. Some of Mary's possessions are here along with period furnishings, and a tour of the house shows how she lived and entertained for the final 17 years of her life.

Mary Washington lived just down the street from her daughter, in the home that George bought for her.

History is found on every street corner in Fredericksburg. **George Washington's Masonic Lodge #4** (803 Princess Anne Street) still stands, and while it's not open to the public it does function for monthly meetings on the second Friday of every month.

Another site worth seeing, if only from the exterior, is the **Lewis Store** on the corner of Caroline and Lewis Streets. Built in 1749 and awaiting restoration, it's one of the oldest urban retail buildings in the United States. The Washington family often shopped here, and George's sister married the founder's son.

George Washington's Masonic Lodge #4 is one of many local landmarks found throughout historic Fredericksburg.

Cross the Rappahannock River by following William Street east and follow the signs to **Ferry Farm**, the boyhood home of George Washington. When the Washington family lived here in the 18th century, it was on the very edge of the frontier.

Some of our favorite legends about young George originated in this place, and you can take a self-guided tour of the 80-plus acres and ponder the life of the man who would become our first president.

Fredericksburg boasts dozens of dining options. **Eileen's Bakery and Café** (1115 Caroline Street) has the distinction of being housed in a circa 1833 Reformed Baptist Church, offering heavenly breads, pastries, cakes, cookies, salads, soups and sandwiches every day except Mondays.

The Capital Ale House (917 Caroline Street) is found in a 200-year-old building that has been stylishly updated while retaining its historic character. Certified Angus Beef, fresh seafood, poultry, and vegetarian dishes are on the menu, along with beer. Lots and lots of beer.

Over 62 craft and imported beers are on tap, and 300 are available by the bottle. Bring your growler for a refill – a sudsy souvenir of the day in Fredericksburg.

FYI:

- Take this day trip on a Saturday to enjoy all its elements.
- A helpful visitors' guide is available at www.visitfred.com.
- Most museums are open daily and closed on major holidays.
- Find more info at www.fredericksburgvacations.com.
- The Timeless Ticket is worth the cost if you plan to visit several attractions.

Carpe Weekend's tip:

Fishing is allowed at Ferry Farm. Anglers must have a valid Virginia fishing license and obtain a permit from the Visitors Center before heading down to the river and casting a line.

JEB Stuart commands traffic in one of the circles on Monument Avenue.

White House of the Confederacy: A jarring reminder

The meticulously restored home of Jefferson Davis, president of the Confederate States of America, is a bit incongruous with its surroundings. Smack dab in the middle of a bustling medical center in Richmond with the Civil War 150 years in the past, it looks as though it's been deposited there by a time machine.

The juxtaposition of the **White House of the Confederacy** with its modern backdrop has garnered criticism from some visitors. But consider that this stately Southern mansion – a part of the indelible history of all Americans – is tucked on its parcel of land amid a place of healing in a state where much of the fighting took place. Then consider that 150 years is not all that long ago, in the grand scheme of things.

The White House of the Confederacy (1201 E. Clay Street) was the social and political epicenter of Richmond, Virginia during the War Between the States. A guided tour, combined with a visit to its companion museum, gives a glimpse at the lives of the people of the South – from the president and his generals to the soldiers and their families.

A docent leads you through the home on an engaging tour that shares the history of the building, from its construction in 1818 for $20,000 through to its present-day reincarnation as a National Historic Landmark.

Eleven rooms are displayed, and all have been restored to their appearance at the time of the Civil War. Furniture and items (except for the textiles) are original to the period, and many were owned by Jefferson Davis and his family.

The rosewood table in the dining room is original, and it was here that the Confederate president met with Robert E. Lee and other key figures to discuss strategy. You can't help but wish these walls could talk.

On a lighter note, the small cannon in the children's room is not a toy; it's a piece of miniature artillery owned by Davis' five-year-old son. The story goes that he was allowed to play with it in the house until he loaded it up with gunpowder, outfitted it with teensy-tiny fuses and fired.

The garden outside is faithfully maintained through the generosity of the President Davis Chapter of the United Daughters of the Confederacy. It's a great place to transition back to the present day, take a few photos and digest what you've seen.

The White House of the Confederacy is now surrounded by a bustling Virginia Commonwealth University Medical Center.

Just next door, the **Museum of the Confederacy** takes a look at the Confederate soldiers and families – boasting the world's most comprehensive collection of Confederate artifacts in its three floors of unique exhibits.

The flagship exhibit, *The Confederate Years,* serves as an excellent primer for those of us who weren't quite paying attention in history class. Civil War buffs will also enjoy it for its depth and level of detail.

One highlight is the rustic headquarters tent of Robert E. Lee. It was said by Lee's chief of staff, Walter Taylor, that Lee was "never so uncomfortable as when he was comfortable."

The treatment for malaria was smuggled inside this unassuming doll.

Numerous flags, including the elegant, restored 4 foot by 5 foot Caroline Grey, are featured. Handcrafted and presented by the ladies of Caroline County, it depicts 36 men in uniform on the reverse side. Curators speculate that the distinct faces could be miniature portraits of the soldiers.

In contrast, a larger-than-life highlight of the museum is *The Last Meeting*, Edward B. D. Julio's 1869 painting of the final encounter of Lee and Jackson. At 15 feet high and 9 feet wide including the frame, it captures a significant moment between the most famous generals of the Confederacy.

Two exhibits on the lower level help bring the war into focus on a more personal note. *The War Comes Home* illustrates how war altered daily life in the South, and at the same time, how life went on.

People still got married and raised children during the period, and the stuff of their lives is on display here. Original copies of *Dixie Children: A Geographical Reader* and *Southern Confederate Arithmetic* make clear that life was abnormally normal.

Knickknackery showcases items that are a bit quirky, including a gnarly prosthetic arm made of boiled leather and a smuggling doll used to transport much-need quinine to the Confederate troops. The Currier and Ives three-way Davis-Lee-Jackson picture is not to be missed, along with POW autograph books, Civil War valentines and a scrapbook that shows the softer side of its owner, JEB Stuart.

On the museum's upper level, *Between the Battles* illustrates how soldiers occupied their idle time when not in combat. Items they made and used are enhanced by photographs and quotes, giving the men a face and a voice.

Not ready to go home yet? Stop by the **Jefferson Hotel** (101 W. Franklin Street) for a spot of tea. Contrary to popular belief, the polished marble staircase at the Jefferson was not used in *Gone with the Wind*. But don't let that stop you from visiting this grand old hotel – it has an illustrious past, nonetheless.

A small display case on the first floor shares the history of this place where John D. Rockefeller, Henry Ford, Charles Lindberg, Charlie Chaplin and Elvis Presley all counted sheep.

The hotel was built in 1895 by Lewis Ginter, who served in the Confederate Army and reached the rank of major. After the war he made partner in an innovative tobacco company, which later became the American Tobacco Company.

The Jefferson's domed glass skylight of Tiffany glass is the original, as is the life-size statue of Thomas Jefferson created by famed Richmond sculptor Edward Valentine. Both works survived a devastating fire that swept through the hotel in 1901. Sadly the statue was beheaded during rescue efforts, but Valentine was able to repair it in his nearby studio.

On the way out of town, drive down **Monument Avenue** – where statues of Jefferson Davis, JEB Stuart, Robert E. Lee, Stonewall Jackson and two additional Richmond residents of note line the street as a prime example of the Grand American Avenue style of city planning.

The architecture of surrounding homes and churches provides a gracious backdrop and an interesting conclusion to a thought-provoking day.

FYI:

- The museum and mansion are closed on holidays.
- A combination admission ticket is available.
- Photography is allowed inside the museum but not the mansion.
- The White House of the Confederacy is not wheelchair accessible.
- Parking at 550 N. 12th Street is validated by the museum.
- Directions to the hotel and monuments are available at the museum.
- Afternoon tea is served by reservation on weekends in the Jefferson's Palm Court. Reservations are required.

Carpe Weekend's tip:

On another day, plan to visit the museum's Appomattox facility – near the Appomattox Court House National Historical Park in Central Virginia – to see General Robert E. Lee's sword, as well as the frock coat he wore at the surrender to General Grant.

Working Point by David Hess is on display at the Museum of Industry.

Elaine C. Jean

Museum of Industry: Ain't no better place than Bal'more

Dedicated to the Industrial Revolution in what was once America's fastest growing city, Baltimore's Museum of Industry recreates a cannery, a machine shop, a printing operation and a garment factory. The only thing missing is the work force that fueled this time in history – with the sweat of its labor and hope for a good life.

The Industrial Revolution in America, spanning most of the 19th century, ushered in a dramatic improvement to the country's standard of living. Suddenly a steady stream of goods was available, a direct result of the shift from making products by hand to mass-producing them by machine. And at the center of it all was Charm City.

Baltimoreans produced just about everything – from underwear to overalls, from automobiles to the bridges that carried them – in what had become the third-largest city in the United States by the year 1820. Merchant ships crammed the harbor and factories lined its docks, all trying to put their stake in a game they thought would never end.

The Museum of Industry (1415 Key Highway) was formerly the home of Landra Beach Platt's 19th century fruit, vegetable and oyster canning plant. The first room you'll likely visit portrays the mood of the factory and explains the local oystering process – from dredging and shucking the bivalves to canning them. A conveyor belt overhead shatters the peace, leading visitors to wonder just how noisy a fully functioning oyster plant might have been.

The museum begs another important question: Why is this fascinating tribute to the region's past so eerily empty? On the day I visited, a handful of visitors wandered around enjoying displays that are so compelling they're almost a form of art.

The time is right to discover Baltimore's Museum of Industry, before everyone else does. Take the free tour – by docent or by iPhone – and visit each room to learn about the industry it represents.

A city full of machinery needed to keep everything in tip-top shape and the museum's working machine shop shows us how. A blacksmith is on hand most Saturdays to explain the works and demonstrate his trade.

Foodies marvel at several exhibits that follow, where period photography and equipment from bygone days in the hot dog industry might make you a bit squeamish. Baltimore was also the home of McCormick Spices, and it's still the home of Domino Sugar.

Display cases detailing the dairy, soda and baking industries are downright nostalgic with pop bottles and memorabilia. A docent tells the story of Hendler's brilliant marketing plan to promote their ice cream by providing local pharmacies with free fountain set-ups – pointing out that ingenuity is a Baltimore product, too.

By 1884 Baltimore was home to 104 printers, and typesetting was bringing about another revolution – the growth of literacy in the United States. The museum's working linotype machine, manned by a printer on Saturdays, illustrates just how labor-intensive the newspaper industry was in a world without computers.

Did you know that Baltimore was once the umbrella capital of the world? Polan Katz boasted umbrellas that were "born in Baltimore and raised everywhere," while the Gans Brothers promised "reigning beauty." By the 20th century Baltimore was producing 1.5 million umbrellas annually, known for their beauty, durability and value.

Perhaps the most interesting feature of the museum is the Baltimore Clothing Company, with its rows of sewing machines. If these Singers could talk, they'd tell of a harsh world of 72-hour work weeks, child labor and sweatshop conditions. Bolts of both blue and gray fabric reveal that Baltimore's factories sometimes sided with the green in the Civil War.

Over 17,000 workers were employed in the 340 companies of Baltimore's clothing industry by 1940, but by 1950 an irreversible downward trend – brought on by synthetics and Japanese imports – had begun. The industry had survived rapid growth, the Depression and labor strikes, but low-cost labor from other countries had finally put the needle trade out of business.

Informative panels on the walls of this room lead to the question: Where do we go from here? Perhaps the greatest benefit of the Museum of Industry is that it helps us better understand America's industrial past as we make decisions about the future.

An antique car and wagon gallery features an Esskay meat truck and a Jacob Fussel ice cream wagon, as well as other vehicles that are uniquely Baltimore. The Appliance Repair Shop is especially appreciated by grandparents on the tour. This is a wonderful multigenerational day trip where elders can tell their grandkids about life before the Internet.

The workroom of the Baltimore Clothing Factory speaks of long, hard days.

History buffs will likely linger at a wall devoted to Maryland's milestones – including the introduction of the first practical submarine, the development of the first transatlantic aircraft and the invention of the world's first aluminum ski. All in … You guessed it … Baltimore.

The iconic Domino Sugar sign may be seen from several vantage points.

Most visitors linger to enjoy the industrial art and historic pieces in the yard. *Working Point* by David Hess incorporates 90 tons of obsolete cast iron, steel and concrete from Baltimore's bygone era in an inspiring tribute to the past.

Bethlehem Steel contributed a crane that's retired from the shipyard, having led a patriotic life of repairing the vessels damaged in WWII. The 1906 steam tug *Baltimore*, once used to break up ice in the harbor to allow access by commercial ships, is undergoing restoration here. And the partially submerged hull of the *Gov. R.M. McLane* of Oyster Wars fame rests where she sank, easily viewed from a nearby dock.

The waterfront provides an interesting spot to ponder the day, where the past meets the present under the Domino Sugar sign. Overlooking the Inner Harbor's blend of gritty reality and upscale renovation, you get the feeling that it's true what they say: Ain't no better place than Bal'more!

FYI:

- This trip is best made on a Saturday.
- The museum is closed on Mondays and major holidays.
- Call ahead to confirm the museum has not closed for a private event.
- Admission is reasonable, with discounts for seniors and children.
- The docent-guided tour is free.
- Audio tours are available for iPhone at no additional charge.

Carpe Weekend's tip:

Special events – including July 4th fireworks, wine and beer tastings and a haunted factory tour – are held throughout the year. To see a complete list of activities, visit www.bmi.org.

George Carter converted the mansion at Oatlands from brick Georgian to stucco Greek Revival.

Oatlands Historic Mansion: Welcome South

It's a popular tourist destination, with gardens that are among the most beautiful in Virginia. The history of Oatlands is inextricably tied to the area around it, and a visit will help to connect the dots of Virginia's past while providing a quiet day in the country.

Oatlands Plantation (20850 Oatlands Plantation Lane) in Leesburg is a gentle reminder that we are in the South. Extensive gardens are scented with roses, framed with boxwood and arranged with a lightness and elegance that make even this Bostonian want to reach for a mint julep.

The mansion remains true to former owner George Carter's vision for his home, and tours of the first floor are offered daily. Special events – such as the Middleburg All Breed Dog Show and Christmas at Oatlands – are held throughout the seasons.

But before you visit Oatlands, it's important to understand a bit of the local history.

In 1798, wheat was king. Young George Carter had just won 3,400 acres in a family lottery, and while others might have considered the rural outpost a consolation prize, Carter looked at the wheat dancing in the breeze and envisioned a sea of dollar signs.

The great-grandson of Robert "King" Carter, a man whose wealth was legendary, George planted his home on the tract in 1804 and a thriving community sprung up around it – post office, mill, school and church. It still exists today with the exception of the mill, comprising the Oatlands Historic District.

Carter had great foresight and business acumen, recognizing that, while the surrounding area was indeed a rural outpost, the combination of its location on Goose Creek with a superb growing climate made this prime real estate. The area would later become known as the Breadbasket of the Confederacy.

Meanwhile, down on Goose Creek, land that is now the town of Aldie was once owned by Charles Fenton Mercer. In 1807 Mercer decided to build his grain mill there, a village sprung up around it, and Aldie became a major industrial center in Loudoun County.

Carter's fortune grew, and his Oatlands Mill became even larger than the Aldie Mill – yielding 40 barrels of flour each day. Carter expanded his operations to include other grains, sheep, a gristmill, a saw mill and a vineyard, providing one-stop shopping for clients from miles around.

To extend their reach, Carter and Mercer joined forces and lobbied for a canal that would make Goose Creek navigable from their mills to the Potomac River; but it was not meant to be. The canal only made it about 12 miles up the creek – a far cry from the trip to Oatlands and Aldie – and it was never used for commercial purposes. Even without the canal, Mercer and Carter were two of the richest men in Virginia.

Their prosperity was due largely to the hard work of enslaved African Americans; when George Carter inherited his land, he arrived with 17 slaves. Just prior to the Civil War, that number had grown to 128, making the slave population at Oatlands the largest in Loudoun County.

The mansion was originally built as a Georgian house in 1804, constructed of stately brick. By the late 1820s, Carter had added a three-story Corinthian portico and covered the exterior brick with stucco, transforming it into the Greek Revival mansion you see today. He also added a bank barn, a smokehouse and several other dependencies, including the propagation greenhouse that is one of the oldest in the country.

The next residents of the home, William and Edith Eustis, kept most of the structure true to the Carter era. Just driving down the tree-lined driveway, it's easy to imagine the peace that the Carters, and later the Eustis family, felt on the land they called home.

After purchasing tickets at the circa 1903 **Carriage House**, a Eustis-period addition, you can wander around the grounds and enjoy several acres of formal gardens and connecting terraces before joining a tour of the mansion.

In the early 20th century, after Oatlands was purchased by the Eustis family, Edith Corcoran Eustis promptly made her mark on the plantation's gardens and updated the greenhouse. Today you see the fruits of her labor in the design of the parterres and artful display of tulips, peonies, irises and lilies.

A bowling green and reflecting pool share a long terrace, with Edith's tea house anchoring one side and statuary anchoring the other. The idyllic scene is a highlight of the property.

After leisurely enjoying the gardens and the dependencies, mosey on up to the front porch of the mansion for a guided tour of its first floor. Rooms are restored to either the Carter or Eustis era, giving insight to the lives of the families who lived here.

Among the unexpected treasures is a set of china from George and Martha Washington, as well as a lock of hair from our first president. Take a self-guided tour of the second floor, with interpretive signage to lead the way. Featured is the room where First Lady Eleanor Roosevelt often stayed when she visited Oatlands.

Stop by the gift shop for books, tea accessories, frames, jewelry, artwork, glassware, ornaments, toys, gardening items and Oatlands merchandise – all tasteful and lasting reminders of a great day trip.

FYI:

- Oatlands is open daily from April 1 – December 30.
- The mansion is closed on major holidays.
- Admission is reasonable, with discounts for children and seniors.
- Tickets are sold in the Carriage House.
- Pets are not allowed.

Jonathan Letterman (far left) met with President Lincoln at Antietam on
October 3, 1862.
Detail from a photograph by Alexander Gardner
Courtesy of Library of Congress, Prints & Photographs Division

Battle of Antietam: A cruel mother of invention

The Battle of Antietam took place on September 17, 1862. Commemorate this turning point in the Civil War by visiting Antietam National Battlefield in Maryland, and learn about Jonathan Letterman, Clara Barton and other innovative caregivers and unsung heroes of the day.

Nothing can prepare visitors for the eerie calm of this hallowed ground. Re-enactors quietly gather and, for a split second, appear to have dropped in from the past. Ghosts of the Blue and the Gray surely linger in cornfields and surrounding woods at night, long after tourists have gone home.

Don't know much about the Civil War? That's no reason to shy away from **Antietam National Battlefield** (5831 Dunker Church Road) in Sharpsburg, Maryland. This is a place of learning, of trying to understand the horrific casualties of September 17, 1862.

The Battle of Antietam was the single bloodiest day in American military history. During a 12-hour period of fighting, 23,000 soldiers were killed, wounded or missing as Confederate and Union troops converged in this peaceful farming community.

When the fighting was over, the outcome was declared a draw. But Confederate troops had failed to gain a much-needed stronghold on Northern soil, and Abraham Lincoln soon issued the Emancipation Proclamation declaring all slaves in the South free.

Audiovisual presentations and exhibits in the **Visitors Center** give an overview of the battle. An award-winning film is shown every 30 minutes, with a longer version offered at noon.

Most people drive the recommended route, but hikers and bicyclists are also welcome. The gift shop sells audio programs to enhance the learning opportunity, and rangers are available to answer questions and provide maps to get you started.

Re-enactors often camp at the Newcomer House, which is open to the public.

Visitors seeking a personalized experience can enlist Antietam Battlefield Guides, a service that provides knowledgeable individuals who will drive your car through the park for you. The standard tour lasts less than three hours and must be reserved at (301) 432-4329. Fees vary by the tour and the number of people in the group.

Bonnymeed Farm's popular horse-drawn carriage tours of the battlefield depart from the flagpole at the Visitors Center. For rates and additional information, visit www.bonnymeedfarm.com.

In a restored farmhouse on Antietam Battlefield, **The Pry House Field Hospital Museum** focuses on the field medicine practiced during the battle. The selfless heroes of the war – civilian volunteers, surgeons and caregivers – are honored for their courage and innovative thinking.

While its human toll was unthinkable, the Battle of Antietam did result in new approaches to emergency medical treatment and evacuation that are still in use today, thanks largely to the work of Jonathan Letterman.

In 1862, the home of Phillip Pry was converted to the headquarters of General George B. McClellan and used as a field hospital for Union officers. The general and his entourage lived and camped here and had a perfect view of the battlefield.

McClellan tasked Letterman to organize a new ambulance system for the Army of the Potomac, and so the surgeon devised a plan and gave every regiment horse-drawn ambulances, trained men and necessary equipment.

On September 17, Letterman partially implemented his plan and efficiently evacuated wounded soldiers from Antietam Battlefield to pre-selected field hospitals. As a result, all of the wounded were removed within an unprecedented 36 hours, and a new system was born.

Clara Barton was also at Antietam Battlefield that day, and from her empathy and swift action came advances in the humane treatment of our wounded warriors.

McClellan's headquarters at the Pry House also served as a hospital for officers.

Barton brought fresh medical supplies and clean drinking water to the field hospital at nearby Poffenberger Farm, and she also performed minor surgery on the battlefield with a pocket knife. She went on to establish the American Red Cross in 1881 and served as its president until 1904.

The museum honors the caregivers who tended to soldiers with little regard for their own safety. The operating theater, with its life-size diorama of Letterman performing surgery on General Joseph Hooker, brings the past to life but may be too grisly for young history buffs.

Most visitors enjoy the debunking of famous myths, such as the misconception that Civil War surgeons were little more than hacks, and that their anesthesia of choice was a bullet between the molars. The truth is that most amputations were entirely necessary, and proper anesthesia was used in 95 percent of the surgeries performed.

America emerged from the medical dark ages as a direct result of what was learned during the Civil War, and the **National Museum of Civil War Medicine** (48 E. Patrick Street) in Historic Frederick, a 30-minute drive from Antietam, serves to illustrate the point.

The National Museum of Civil War Medicine contains life-size dioramas, including this depiction of camp life.

An excellent complement to the Pry House, The National Museum of Civil War Medicine brings into even greater focus the challenges faced by Civil War medical personnel and the innovations that resulted. Exhibits are made personal with the stories of surgeons, medics and nurses, as well as case studies of their patients.

Two floors of informative displays and dioramas of scenes both on and off the battlefield make this a particularly engaging museum for people of all ages and interest levels.

Frederick was once considered a crossroad of the Civil War, and much of the period's architecture survives. Historic Downtown Frederick is also home to several acclaimed restaurants, antique stores and boutiques.

FYI:

- Admission to each of the recommended sites is reasonable.
- The battlefield and museums are open daily but closed on holidays.
- Directions to the Pry House and National Museum of Civil War
  Medicine are available at the Antietam Battlefield Visitors Center.

Carpe Weekend's tip:

An anniversary program is offered in September, and a memorial illumination is held in December.

Robert E. Lee was the last of the Lees to be born at Stratford Hall, later explaining that "Stratford … is endeared to me by many memories."

The slave quarters closest to the Great House were constructed of stone for improved appearance and resistance to fire.

Stratford Hall: The Lee family and their legacy

*A visit to the Northern Neck birthplace of General Robert E. Lee –
named Stratford Hall after his ancestral home in Shropshire, England –
offers a tranquil day trip along Virginia's roads less traveled.*

Touring **Stratford Hall** (483 Great House Road), you'll learn about the
five generations of Lees who lived here, and of the profound impact that
early members had on the beginning of our young republic. The nation
they helped to forge proved so strong that even the bloodiest conflict in
American history would not destroy it.

Founding Father and President John Adams once remarked that the Lees
gave us "more men of merit than any other family," having produced two
signers of the Declaration of Independence, one governor of the Virginia
Colony and a distinguished Revolutionary War commander. But it is
largely for the role in history one Lee played during the Civil War that
the name is remembered today.

Robert Edward Lee came into the world in the bed chamber of the stately
Southern plantation home on January 19, 1807, but he lived at Stratford
Hall for less than four years before his father, Henry "Light-Horse
Harry" Lee, relocated the family to Alexandria.

The Lees had fallen on hard times, and after Light-Horse Harry died his
son could not afford a university education. So the future general
garnered an appointment to the US Military Academy at West Point, and
there his career began.

Lee proved himself worthy, earning three honorary field promotions in
the Mexican War and becoming an officer in the Corps of Engineers, as
well as the Superintendent of West Point; but he is most famous as
commander of the Confederate Army of Northern Virginia. After the

Civil War, Lee was named president of what is now Washington and Lee University in Lexington, Virginia.

But from 1807 to 1810, Robert E. Lee wasn't any of those things; he was a little boy enjoying a few short years in the house he would always call home. Built in the 1730s by great-uncle Thomas Lee, Stratford Hall was once a thriving plantation, a self-sufficient community that produced tobacco, wheat, barley, oats, flax and corn.

Stratford Hall was acquired by Mrs. Charles Lanier of Louisville in 1929 and is now owned and operated by the Robert E. Lee Memorial Association. A multi-million dollar restoration is in the works to restore several rooms to their late 18th century appearance.

Tickets for a guided tour of the mansion may be purchased in the **Stetson Building**, where visitors can learn about the Lee family's historical legacies and discover the wide variety of activities available at this 1,900-acre plantation. Most sightseers are surprised to learn that they can collect sharks teeth and fossils by walking along the small strip of beach adjacent to the grist mill.

A wood and steel bridge leads to the historic area, crossing a deep ravine – and the past two centuries. A docent will guide you through the house, which was built from 600,000 bricks that were made on the plantation from its clay and oyster shells and then rubbed by the hands of its slaves.

Two meticulously recreated stone buildings housed the families of enslaved people who worked in or near the **Great House**. The living quarters you see today are remarkable for both their level of detail and the insight they provide about the people who were the lifeline of the plantation's economy.

During a guided tour of the Great House, a docent shares stories about the lives of all five generations of Lees. You'll see an impressive collection of American and English decorative arts that combine family pieces, period pieces and reproductions.

The **Great Hall**, resplendent in Georgian symmetry, has been described as one of the most beautiful rooms in America. You'll be invited to take a seat and listen to a brief background of the family and its home before being escorted through the mansion. Of special note is the room in which Robert E. Lee was born over 200 years ago.

While you'll visit formal rooms that are absolutely gorgeous, it's the utilitarian spaces that are fascinating. The school room, wet and dry stores, spinning and weaving area, kitchen, wine cellar and laundry room illustrate the complexity of working life on an 18th century plantation.

In 1935 the plantation was dedicated by the Robert E. Lee Memorial Association as a tribute to the Lees. Stratford Hall now tells the remarkable story of the Lee family, their home and their impact on American history.

FYI:

- Stratford Hall is currently open on weekends and holidays.
- Tickets for a tour of the Great House are reasonably priced.
- Hours vary by season; check www.stratfordhall.org.
- Tours begin at 10 a.m. Arrive 15 minutes early to buy tickets.
- The Plantation Store sells gifts, books, honey, drinks and snacks.

Carpe Weekend's tip:

Admission is free every year on Robert E. Lee's birthday, January 19.

Norton, our Goldendoodle and best buddy, enjoys Yappy Hour
in the Hotel Monaco's courtyard.

5. FIDO-FRIENDLY FUN

Old Town Alexandria, Virginia: Dog days of summer

They're our very best friends, our walking companions and our therapists. We tuck them into bedazzled hand bags, dress them up in raincoats and galoshes and prune them like so much topiary at Disney World. And yet our dogs love us. Unconditionally.

This day trip gives proper thanks to our loyal canine companions.

Begin by grabbing a bench in front of **The Dairy Godmother** (2310 Mount Vernon Avenue) in Alexandria's Del Ray neighborhood, where Wisconsin-style frozen custard rules. Here Puppy Pops come in two flavors – pumpkin and banana – and are made with doggie digestive systems in mind from peanut butter and plain yogurt. Best of all, 10 cents from every pop sold goes to a charity that benefits animal companions.

Humans enjoy dense, smooth frozen custard in chocolate and vanilla, as well as the flavor-of-the-day. Sorbets capture the essence of the season and contain no fat, dairy products or eggs. The Godmother is also known for light and luscious homemade marshmallows – treats that will have you coming back, begging for more.

Virginia's **Old Town Alexandria** is one of the most dog-friendly shopping districts in America, with several stores that set out bowls of water, offer treats and even welcome your best friend to step inside. After an afternoon of hoofing it, visit the **Dog Park** (705 King Street). Dogs will appreciate a break from the heat, and you'll love the selection of collars, bowls, toys and treats. Buy a few cookies in the shape of palm trees, starfish and ice cream cones for an on-the-spot reward that celebrates good weather.

Just around the corner (139 S. Fairfax Street), **The Enchanted Florist** offers doggie treats from a charming wooden dispenser on its stretch of sidewalk real estate. Floral arrangements and gifts for the humans in your life are found inside.

Treat time: Norton's favorite part of the Canine Cruise.

Join in the fun during Yappy Hour at the **Hotel Monaco** (480 King Street). It's a well-known fact that the folks on the opposite end of a leash tend to be friendly, but those who congregate in the courtyard at the

Hotel Monaco every Tuesday and Thursday evening from April through October are the happiest around. Locals mingle with guests while dogs perform the requisite sniff tests, and most are on their best behavior.

At the Hotel Monaco there's usually at least one entertainer in the crowd.

If you shy away from off-leash parks, this is the place for you – socializing your tethered pet while sipping an adult beverage and enjoying Jackson 20's snacks is very civilized, indeed. Tavern bites include market oysters, shrimp salad, burgers, ribs, a charcuterie board and a cheese sampler. The BBQ pork sliders, deviled eggs, fried green tomatoes, J20 fries and house-made tater tots are specially priced for Yappy Hour.

Each pup is given a bowl of water and free treats by a friendly staff that fawns over him as if he were royalty. A few rules apply to keep things fun for everyone; visit www.monaco-alexandria.com for details.

You'll want to stay until the crowd disperses, but don't yield to temptation. There's still plenty to do during this day that's all about dogs.

The Torpedo Factory Art Center (105 N. Union Street) has long been recognized as a haven for the creative, with more than 80 studios, six galleries, the Art League School and the Archaeological Museum. But did you know the Torpedo Factory welcomes well-behaved, leashed dogs? Some artists produce pet portraits, so you can commission a lasting souvenir of this dog-friendly day trip.

The Torpedo Factory stays open late on Thursday nights and welcomes dogs.

The Potomac Riverboat Company's Canine Cruise departs at designated times from the dock behind the Torpedo Factory. Every Thursday evening dozens of dogs embark on a journey – that's remarkably free of barking – around Alexandria's seaport. Tour guides point out important landmarks and share local lore, while humans and canines kick back and enjoy a cool breeze off the water.

The cruise lasts 40 minutes, and tickets are free for pawed passengers and reasonable for their human companions. Since this is a popular event, advance purchases are highly recommended and may be made online at www.potomacriverboatco.com. Tickets are also sold at the company's kiosk on the waterfront.

When the dog days of summer are upon you, treat your canine companion to a vacation day to thank him for all he does. After all, where would we be without our furry friends? And, as comedian George Carlin once quipped, "It's not right to make a dog just lie around on his day off – that's his regular job!"

FYI:

- This trip is best enjoyed on a Thursday evening in the summer.
- Dogs must be well-behaved and connected to a 6-foot leash.
- The usual clean-up rules apply.
- The Dairy Godmother is closed on Mondays and Tuesdays.
- Admission to the Torpedo Factory is free.
- For a complete list of dog friendly stores and eateries, consult www.visitalexandriava.com.

The past meets the present on Duke of Gloucester Street in Williamsburg.

Williamsburg: Dogs love DOG Street

Do you believe in ghosts? If you and your best friend love to sniff out a mystery, visit Duke of Gloucester Street in Williamsburg, Virginia. By day it's a pet-friendly destination that takes you back in time, but in the evening it may just bring you to a whole 'nother dimension.

When it comes to Colonial history, no one does it better than Williamsburg: More than 300 acres of 18th century living and learning, garnished with enough brick, ivy, candles and formal gardens to make the Redcoats surrender to our impeccable taste.

But this town of elegance and order has a dark side, and the **Original Ghosts of Williamsburg Candlelight Tour** brings it out of hiding. Although there are several ghost tours operating in town, this one is highly recommended for its lively storytelling and documented tales.

When you get into the area stop by the **Williamsburg General Store** (1656 Richmond Road) to buy tickets for a tour on the same night. Or, better yet, purchase them online at www.theghosttour.com. The cost is reasonable for adults and free for kids under the age of six, as well as for canines of all ages.

During the remainder of the day poke around and explore the past, since dogs are welcome outdoors at all three sites in the **Historic Triangle**.

An admission fee gains seven-day access to **Historic Jamestowne**. Found at the western end of the Colonial Parkway, this was the location of the first successful English colony in America. Dogs are allowed on the grounds and not in the buildings, but you'll still get the flavor of the era through a number of activities, re-enactments and events.

Fast forward about 170 years by driving to the other end of the Colonial Parkway. **Yorktown Battlefield** also welcomes pets on the grounds, and admission is included in the price of the aforementioned pass. It was here that British troops surrendered in 1781, effectively ending the American Revolutionary War.

If there is still daylight to be had, stroll along **Duke of Gloucester Street** in the heart of **Colonial Williamsburg** and enjoy the sights, starting in **Merchants Square**.

Hungry yet? **The Cheese Shop** (410 W. Duke of Gloucester Street) makes sandwiches and salads to order, along with cheese and charcuterie boards. Browse the menu online and call in your order at (757) 220-0298; the meal will be ready for pick-up from an outdoor window, and tables are conveniently located in front of the building.

An admission fee is not required to walk down Duke of Gloucester Street, affectionately called DOG by the locals, but donations are accepted. Note that Fido isn't welcome inside any of the buildings, despite the pineapples of hospitality that abound.

Shadows play tricks with a healthy imagination in Williamsburg after sundown.

Hoofing it along the main thoroughfare brings you through the restored area, a round-trip journey of about two miles. You'll see the Governor's Palace, Capitol, Courthouse, Blacksmith Shop, Printing Office and

Magazine, as well as the home of Peyton Randolph, one of Virginia's leading politicians. This is reportedly the most haunted building in Williamsburg, and you'll learn more about it later in the evening.

Participants convene 15 minutes before each scheduled tour in front of the **College of William and Mary Bookstore** (345 W. Duke of Gloucester Street). Together you'll trek across the campus of the university as well as over much of Duke of Gloucester Street, so wear walking shoes and bring an umbrella for seasonal showers.

Our guide was animated and well versed in the history of the area, and he presented the stories of L.B. Taylor, author of *The Ghosts of Williamsburg*, *The Ghosts of Tidewater* and other spine-tingling tales. When the evening begins, it's all light-hearted fun. But by the end of the night, even skeptics are seeing dead people.

That's not to say it's terrifying … There are usually kids in the group, and they don't tend to be the least bit daunted. Some of us might actually want to believe – especially when Halloween is fast approaching and leaves crunch underfoot. It is Williamsburg, after all. But that doesn't explain some of the anomalies that may make themselves known in photos from the evening.

FYI:

- Carry a water dish and refill it from public restrooms around town.
- Always bring disposable bags so you can clean up after your dog.
- Use a leash at all times; it's the law.
- Purchase tickets in the Williamsburg General Store or at www.theghosttour.com.

Carpe Weekend's tip:

Rather than drive home late at night, you may opt to stay at the **LaQuinta Inn** (814 Capitol Landing Road). It's not exactly LaQuainta, but they do allow pets in the rooms.

Built in 1875, Currituck Lighthouse was the last beacon to be added to OBX.

The Outer Banks: Not quite ruffing it

Each year 7 million visitors flock to the Outer Banks with kids, campers and kayaks in tow. Sadly, our furry friends are often left behind. But OBX – and many of its beaches that stretch from the Virginia border to Okracoke Island in North Carolina – may be out to change all that.

Several well-established companies – such as Sun Realty, Southern Shores Realty and Beach Realty – offer rental houses that are pet friendly, and the Sanderling Resort in Duck has designated some of the rooms of their North Inn as fine for Fido, too.

The towns of **Duck** and **Corolla** make a great base camp for travelers with dogs, since many of the beaches allow romping on the sand year round. There are enough activities for human members of the family that you'll want to make this a three-day weekend or a week-long adventure.

After settling in your comfy vacation hideaway, get your lay of this beautiful land with a quick cruise around. One of the first things you'll learn is that boardwalks abound.

Those of us with dogs know that they often explore the world by sniffing it, trampling it and tasting it, so these raised wooden walkways bring our pets into areas where they might not otherwise be allowed. What better way to enjoy nature without making much of an impact?

The **Currituck Heritage Park** in Corolla offers 39 acres of grounds to walk with your leashed pet, and you can view the Currituck Beach Light Station and Whalebone Club Historic Site from the exterior.

A boardwalk leads through marsh and over to the Sound, and a trail leads to **Historic Corolla Village** where a one-room schoolhouse has been converted to a museum that's dedicated to the wild horses of Corolla.

Dogs and SUVs love to run along designated OBX beaches.

If you'd like to make your own search for wild horses, you'll have to hit the beach accessible at the north end of Route 12. There you can drive a 4x4 vehicle all the way to the Virginia border, peering into the dunes for signs of the descendants of mustangs that once belonged to 16th century Spanish explorers. The wild horses can be elusive, so pack plenty of food and water for both the humans and canines onboard if you are on a quest to spot them.

The **Currituck Banks Coastal Estuarine Reserve** – on the return trip just one mile down on the left after you exit the 4x4 beach – is a collage of sand dunes, swales, marshes and forests along the Currituck Sound. A level boardwalk affords the opportunity to walk across brackish swamp without wading through it.

You can observe maritime and swamp forests along the way and spot salamanders and tree frogs in their natural habitat. Then enjoy a vantage point on the Currituck Sound at the end of the trail, where blue heron, snowy egret and other birds gracefully fish for their dinner.

The maritime forest trail makes a side trip off the boardwalk and into woods that deer and fox call home. Follow the blue trail posts beyond the short set of stairs to the left and about a half-mile down the boardwalk as you exit from the sound. If you decide to take the mile-plus detour into the forest, remember to check all hikers for ticks when you are done. And let's not forget the real reason you chose the Outer Banks – sun, sand and surf. The beaches of Duck and Corolla – and some of the establishments – welcome pets with open arms. Literally.

Robin Carey, co-owner of the **Outer Barks** store at the Scarborough Lane Shoppes in Duck, got down on all fours to romp with Norton. Her 2,000 square foot shop has a huge selection of everything your dog needs for a great vacation. Especially popular are bully sticks and pizzle chews made from the desiccated organs of other animals, handy if you want to keep the security deposit on your rental house intact. Don't ask about the previous lives of these natural doggie treats, though, unless you have a strong stomach and don't embarrass easily.

With over 300 miles of coastline, OBX offers plenty of sand, sun and surf.

Outer Barks also sells pet-themed tee-shirts, bumper stickers and gift items, so human companions won't feel left out. But make no mistake: At this shop, pets reign supreme. Check out their website for a schedule of weekly Yappy Hours that include frozen doggie daiquiris, puppy pasta and cake, as well as paw painting, puppy pools and an agility course. They also offer online shopping, so you can continue to visit after the vacation is over.

Norton sniffs out OBX pet stores, begging treats from shop to shop.

Steamers Shellfish to Go in the Tim Buck II Shopping Center on Route 12 in Corolla is the perfect stop for lunch, dinner or takeout. Their fried shrimp, clam, oyster and scallop boats are reminiscent of New England, and lunch and dinner offerings are a cut above typical fish shack fare.

Steamers also sells ribs, chicken and crab cakes, as well as complete steamer pots to go – including potatoes, corn and your choice of shellfish. Just bring them back to the house, add water and turn up the heat for your own clambake.

Picnic tables facing Currituck Sound overlook a paddle boat lagoon, putt-putt golf course and mini-raceway, and leashed dogs are welcome on the deck. After the kids have scarfed down their meals, they can play while you hang out and have a cold one with your very best friend.

The boardwalk behind Tim Buck II is a great place for stretching legs after eating. For the nature lover or photographer there's an osprey nest off to the right and through the trees. That's the great thing about the

Outer Banks; you never really forget that you're a visitor here, with daily evidence of nature's year round residents at every turn.

As you drive along the chain of barrier islands, don't be shy about asking if your dog can join you at restaurants and coffee shops that feature outdoor seating. Our experience has been that pets are welcome more times than they are not. The Outer Banks is a casual vacation destination that's quickly becoming a great place to enjoy with your canine companions – just for the howl of it.

FYI:

- When you really need a recharge, this makes a great extended trip.
- To enjoy all its elements, take this trip between May and October.

Carpe Weekend's tips:

- Be mindful that paws burn easily on hot sand and pavement.
- Keep pets out of the wild grass, where they can pick up burs and ticks.
- Dog policies vary by beach.
- Visit www.outer-banks.nc.us for the latest rules and regs.

Norton and Nikki dig the comfy sofa at Lost Dog Coffee.

Shepherdstown: Steeped in history, not stuck there

Shepherdstown is one dog-friendly, dog-gone-happy, quietly hip, historic little town – just over the West Virginia border but miles away from the madness of two metropolitan areas. Unique shops and restaurants line German Street, and folks stroll without a care.

After a day of exploring this delightful destination, I had to wonder why I hadn't visited before. Perhaps it's all in the marketing and could be easily remedied with a new slogan: *Shepherdstown – Alexandria light!* or *Why not West Virginia?*

Or maybe those of us who have had the good fortune to stumble upon this gem should follow the prime directive and leave her be, because stardom would surely change her. But, there's no harm in a little day tripping …

Shepherdstown is reminiscent of certain Colorado mountain towns – free-spirited, pleasantly worn, edgy without trying to be – with a touch of granola crunch. Even if you're not into history or out looking for it, it will find you. The past bubbles up to the surface like **Town Run** itself.

Yes, Town Run. That's the waterway that's fed by over 20 natural springs before it enters the south side of town. It never floods, and it never runs dry. Town Run meanders through backyards, over alleys, under streets and buildings. Locals speak of it as if it's a living thing, and maybe it is.

The springs have fed the local economy since 1734, when the town was settled. Its water supported the endeavors of tanners, millers, potters and other artisans, and so the population swelled to more than 1,000 by the year 1775.

Did you know … James Rumsey invented the first steamboat in Shepherdstown, and he tested it in the Potomac River in 1787, a full 20 years before Robert Fulton launched the Clermont? The **Rumsey Monument** is found at the end of Mill Street, in a small park with an expansive view of the river, the mountains and the C&O Canal towpath.

Civil War history runs deep. When the Battle of Antietam was fought nearby, more than 5,000 Confederate soldiers retreated to Shepherdstown. Every home, shop, pub, church, alley and street – every nook and cranny of the small town – was filled with the dead and dying.

Shepherd University lends that unmistakable college-town feel, and at the edge of the campus you can see the area's smallest house. Built by the school in 1929, the diminutive dwelling on Princess Street measures 10 feet high by 9 ½ feet wide and was used as a laboratory for observing kids at play.

The **Visitors Center** in the Entler Hotel (129 E. German Street) houses a replica of Rumsey's Steamboat and provides brochures on the area. Perhaps the most helpful is *Historic Shepherdstown: A Walking Tour*. Stop by and grab this essential guide if you would like to explore the Shepherdstown of old.

But while Shepherdstown is steeped in history, it's by no means stuck in the past. Shops offering everything from clothing and toys to arts and crafts line German Street. Here you can buy fine wine, rent a bike or kayak and shop for unusual gifts. Nothing seems to break the bank, and it feels good to support a small town's economy.

One standout is the **German Street Coffee and Candlery** (103 W. German Street), specializing in bath and kitchen items in addition to a variety of chocolate-covered treats – pretzels, espresso beans and the usual suspects, as well as Twinkies on a stick. Gourmet coffee beans and loose teas are also featured, along with wines and cheeses.

Restaurants abound, most notably the Press Room and the Yellow Brick Bank, but I settled into in to the sunken patio of the **Blue Moon Cafe** (200 E. High Street) because it's so … Shepherdstown. And because they welcomed my Goldendoodle puppy.

There is something endearing about a restaurant that allows four-legged friends and has a river running through it. The quaint setting of the Blue

Moon and its homemade vegetarian offerings give the place a peace-love-happiness feel, and stairs sculpted from trees remind us that West Virginia is the home of the mountain arts.

Lost Dog Coffee, (134 E. German Street), is a trip in every sense of the word. Garth Janssen, proprietor and barista, is usually there to offer coffee and quips. Garth muses about whether one can actually own a place or if it owns you. But he seems incredibly happy, so whichever it is it surely works for him.

Garth claims to be striving for a psychotic feng shui, and his efforts show. Visit the pin wall – his version of PostSecret – and read the bathroom to take the pulse of Shepherdstown. Feel free to bring your leashed dog inside the building, "So long as it's well behaved and doesn't pee or bite anyone."

On the day I visited Shepherdstown, a local artist was enthusiastically creating huge, colorful canvases – making him part painter and part performance artist – while sharing a warm smile and kind words. And this is exactly why I traipse around small towns to begin with.

FYI:

- Town Run is the Falling Spring Branch of the Potomac River.
- Metered, on-street parking is available; it's free on Sundays.
- Lost Dog Coffee is not to be confused with Lost Dog Café.
- The Blue Moon Café is open daily; its pub often features live music.

Sky Meadows State Park's road less traveled was yesteryear's thoroughfare.

Delaplane: Hoof it at Sky Meadows, woof it at BOW

*Grab Fido and the family and hop in the car for a day of R&B –
recreation and bonding – in the beautiful countryside of Northern
Virginia. This trip begins with gourmet food, takes you on a brisk walk in
historic woods and ends at a winery that's kid and pet friendly.*

Start the day at the **Locke Modern Country Store** (2049 Millwood
Road) – just over the Clarke County line in the tiny village of Millwood.
Locke has it all – coffee and scones for breakfast, lunch for the trail and
homemade chicken pot pie for dinner. A visit will have you seriously
considering the village life.

Gourmet sandwiches such as the Powerhouse – roasted chicken with
sprouts, carrots, lettuce, tomatoes, avocado and Havarti on multigrain
bread – provide fuel for the hike and are large enough to split. Cookies as
big as saucers could easily be shared, but why? Locke sells chips, water
and other beverages to round out your picnic, and soup, comfort foods
and salads if you'd rather return for a more substantial meal.

Whenever possible, Locke offers locally grown foods that support
sustainability. Established in1836 on land that was once owned by
Robert "King" Carter, this hidden gem is across the street from the 225-
year-old **Burwell-Morgan Mill**.

Going for a hike is enjoyable at almost any time of year, but late-winter
hiking – on those precious days when the moderate, Mid-Atlantic climate
begins to flirt with spring – has benefits of its own. The leaf-free, insect-
light, people-scarce period that some call the brown season offers an
opportunity to see this corner of Northern Virginia in a whole new way.
Uncluttered. Monochromatic. Peaceful.

Photographers love it, depressed people hate it and you can appreciate it
at **Sky Meadows State Park** (11012 Edmonds Lane) in Delaplane. Here

meadows stretch up to forests that stretch up to the Appalachian Trail. That's a lot of stretching, but there are less strenuous trails for hikers of all ages and condition levels.

Hikes in Sky Meadows State Park begin at Bleak House and the nearby Visitors Center, where trail maps are available.

A reasonable admission fee is charged per vehicle – cash only – and the road leads to a parking area next to **Bleak House**, so named for its perch on a wind-swept hill. Built in 1840 by Abner Settle, the postmaster of nearby Paris, it was home to his family from the 1840s to the 1860s.

The house was later owned by a member of Mosby's Rangers and, although no battles were fought on this land, the surrounding countryside was host to Civil War encampments. Trail maps and information about the history of the park may be found at the **Visitors Center**, which is located behind Bleak House.

Trails are a short distance away and lead to sweeping vistas along historic roads. Highly recommended for families and dog owners is the **Boston Mill Road** and **Snowden Interpretive Trail Circuit**.

The wide, hard-packed trail was once the route between the village of Paris and the two gristmills on Crooked Run. Beyond the handcrafted stonewall is a field where wheat and corn were grown, which was then sent to be ground at Simper's Mill and shipped back in barrels as flour. In the 19th century, this was definitely not the road less traveled.

Less than a half-mile straight ahead, rustic stairs lead to the Snowden Trail, a one-mile loop that's well marked with interpretive signage about the habitat and history of the area. The going is easy, yet you will still be rewarded with interesting views and great bird watching.

The park is known for its population of woodpeckers, and butterflies abound in warm weather. The Visitors Center offers free brochures about the flora and fauna of the region and features a new Educational Habitat Room, as well as the gift shop stocked with books about insects, plants, flowers, wildlife and camping. Restrooms are in this building.

Sky Meadows State Park was established in 1975 with the gift of 1,132 acres by Paul Mellon, and it opened in 1983 when the Commonwealth of Virginia completed its accommodations for the public. In 1987 a swath of land containing three miles of the Appalachian Trail was added, and Paul Mellon contributed another 462 acres in 1991. The latter contains a parcel that was once owned by George Washington.

This peaceful scene may be enjoyed on a hike in the brown season.

Now that the kids and the dog have been hiked and fed and everyone's all tuckered out, you could go home. Or you could drive south on Route 17 and follow the signs to **Barrel Oak Winery** (3623 Grove Lane), found near Route 66.

Dogs mix and mingle while their humans taste the wines of BOW.

Perched atop another windswept hill – but by no means bleak – Barrel Oak Winery welcomes you to bring your party to theirs. They provide the wine, and you bring the picnic, kids, dogs, laughter and friends. Bring your own games, break out the house set of bocce balls or join in a rousing game of corn hole.

The tasting room is quite large, and an outdoor seating area is also open on warmer days. Dogs really are welcome with open arms (and sometimes doggie biscuits) into the building, on the patio and on the lawns. A few Doghaus Rules apply, most importantly that you clean up after your pets and keep them on leashes at all times.

But make no mistake: Barrel Oak Winery is all about its award-winning wines.

Their 2010 Viognier won a double gold medal in the American Wine Society's 2011 Commercial Wine Competition, and the 2009 Merlot took silver at the 2011 Tasters Guild International Wine Competition. You can taste six different wines for a small fee and purchase your favorite one by the bottle or the glass.

On most weekends the vineyard is alive with friendly faces and wagging tails, gathered inside the winery and around wood-burning fire bowls on the patio. Grab a glass of Chocolate Lab – a port-style Chambourcin infused with cocoa essence – for the perfect end to the day.

FYI:

- This trip is appropriate for any time of year.
- The Locke Modern Country Store is closed on Mondays.
- Sky Meadows State Park is open until sunset every day.
- Pets must be kept on a leash no longer than six feet.
- Clean-up rules apply.
- Alcohol is not permitted in state parks (except inside tents).
- Outside food is allowed at Barrel Oak Winery.

Canine companions are welcome every day at Sugarloaf Mountain Vineyard.

Sugarloaf Mountain: Savor the moment

This day trip is all about the good life. It's about meeting strangers you have everything in common with ... About savoring a strawberry that tastes as good as it looks ... About sipping wine and soaking in the sunshine, same as the grapes that made it. Most importantly, it's about going on a hike with your family and your very best friend.

Maryland's **Sugarloaf Mountain** sits dependably off in the distance – that mound you see as you drive to the grocery store, run to pick up the kids from karate class and whisk the dog to the groomer. It's the hike you always mean to take – so close and yet so far.

Until now. This weekend, why not pack a cooler full of sandwiches, throw the dog and the kids in the car and skip the grocery shopping? With this trip, you can have your veggies and eat them, too.

If you're coming from Virginia and **White's Ferry** (off James Monroe Highway is Leesburg) is operational, that route sets the stage for an idyllic day trip. Country roads lead past farmhouses and open pastures and up to **Sugarloaf Mountain Vineyard** in Dickerson (18125 Comus Road), one of Maryland's most celebrated wineries.

During the months of May through October, the vineyard hosts a **Farmers Market** on Saturdays from 10 a.m. to 2 p.m. You may want to stop here twice – once in the morning to fuel the hike with fresh fruit and a croissant, and again in the early afternoon to make up for that lost trip to the grocery store.

The entrance to Sugarloaf Mountain is just beyond the winery – as the road forks, it's to the near right. Rules of the park are posted, and trail maps are available.

You can hike to your heart's content on trails that rise 800 feet above the nearby countryside and 1,282 feet above sea level. These circuit hikes are for varying skill levels, so nobody has to be left out.

Technically speaking Sugarloaf is a monadnock, having remained after the erosion of the surrounding land. Its shape prompted pioneers and hunters to name it for the loaves of sugar it resembled.

The mountain is of historical significance, having held lookout posts for both Union and the Confederate armies during the Civil War. A log cabin that still stands at the base served as a makeshift hospital for wounded soldiers.

Wildflowers bloom during the warmer weather, and a variety of forest birds – the great horned owl, wild turkey, red-shouldered hawk and pileated woodpecker – make this their home.

Sugarloaf Mountain is owned and managed by Stronghold, Inc., a private organization established by Gordon and Louise Strong in 1946 to protect and share Sugarloaf's natural beauty. The Strong Mansion has been restored and is now used for weddings and special events.

Picnic tables near the **Potomac Overlook**, **East View** and **West View** parking lots provide a place for a meal with a view. And, after everyone is well fed and ready to turn back, you'll see the beauty of our master plan. That empty cooler is just begging to be filled with fresh herbs and artisanal cheeses, isn't it?

Strolling along the handful of vendors back at the winery, it quickly becomes apparent that this is not your ordinary Farmer's Market. Some share samples, and most are willing to tell you about their philosophies with great enthusiasm. All appear to be living their dreams.

Maybe you've never met these folks before, but they couldn't possibly be called strangers. They've made it their lives' work to put interesting food on your table – food you'll savor and remember. Purchases are usually accompanied by a conversation and a big smile.

The collection of vendors on any given Saturday may vary but will not disappoint. Fresh flowers are often available, as well as hanging baskets, lettuce bowls and potted herbs.

Artisanal bakers purvey breakfast pastries, cookies the size of saucers, pies glistening with fresh fruit and breads that boast of healthy, grainy goodness. Cheeses, butters and spreads are for sale, expertly crafted from the milk of Holstein and Ayrshire cows.

Early in the season you'll score ripe strawberries and other harbingers of spring – asparagus, onions and pickling cucumbers – and a steady stream of high-quality produce will follow as the months pass.

Two Paws Up, a popular pet store and spa in Historic Downtown Frederick that has dubbed itself the doghouse that even your cat will love, is usually in attendance handing out samples. Their foot-long bully sticks are a bargain and make a great souvenir – the gift that keeps on giving.

While you're there, Sugarloaf Mountain Vineyard invites you to try their award-winning Bordeaux-style wines on the patio or inside the winery. Favorites include Chardonnay, Cabernet Sauvignon and Reserve Cabernet Franc.

Dogs are welcome inside the building, and this is a great destination at any time of year. Visit the winery's website at www.smvwinery.com for information about upcoming events.

FYI:

- Enjoy this day trip on a Saturday morning from May - October.
- Sugarloaf Mountain is open daily until one hour before sunset.
- Admission to the park is free.
- Trail maps are available at the entrance, as well as in the parking lots.
- All dogs must be leashed.
- Sugarloaf Mountain Vineyard is closed on major holidays.

Carpe Weekend's tip:

The winery celebrates Dog Days once a month in season, when the upper patio is open as a dog park until noon and local vendors and speakers come to share information and demonstrations.

Diana, goddess of the hunt, oversees the French Parterre and adds a touch of whimsy to the spectacular grounds of Hillwood Estate.

6. SLICE OF ANOTHER LIFE

Hillwood Estate: Where fabulous lives

What's not to love about a historic American country house that looks like it's from Lifestyles of the Rich and Famous*? Tucked against Rock Creek Park in Northwest Washington, DC, Hillwood Estate, Museum and Gardens is known as, "The place where fabulous lives."*

Marjorie Merriweather Post purchased the 25-acre **Hillwood Estate** (4155 Linnean Avenue NW) in 1955 as a place to live, entertain and showcase her magnificent collection of French and Russian art. When she died it became her luxurious gift to the public, opening in 1977 for all to enjoy. And from the moment you walk through the doors, you really will feel like her guest.

One of the wealthiest women in America, she inherited the Postum Cereal Company from her father in 1914 and immediately took an active role in its operations. Post enjoyed a passion for the French decorative arts, and by the time her first marriage ended in 1919 she had been bitten by the collecting bug. Her impeccable taste, desire and means allowed her to assemble the dazzling array of French furniture, tapestry and artwork that we can all enjoy today.

During her second marriage, to businessman Edward F. Hutton, her fortune grew as the company became the General Foods Corporation. The marriage didn't last – perhaps when E.F. Hutton talked she just didn't care to listen – and Post stepped up to join the Board of Directors.

Hillwood Estate, viewed from across the Lunar Lawn, is a treasure trove of French and Russian artifacts.

With her third marriage came the opportunity that would forever change the path of her life and legacy. Husband Joseph E. Davies was the American ambassador to Russia, and during their time in Moscow Post gathered a tremendous amount of Russian imperial art. This set a foundation upon which she continued to build long after she had returned home, divorced Davies and purchased Hillwood Estate.

From the very start, Post knew that she was transforming Hillwood into both a home for herself and a museum for her treasures. She worked with renowned architects and designers to create spaces that are both elegant and welcoming, so while the estate is over-the-top gorgeous it doesn't feel the least bit stuffy.

If you arrive early in the day, your welcome will begin with a conveniently located, free parking space just outside the **Visitors Center**. If you're not so early, that's okay; you'll just be given directions and instructed to park somewhere nearby. Be mindful that on-street parking in the neighborhood around Hillwood is not allowed.

The Visitors Center is large and full of resources to make your visit a success. You can watch a 15-minute orientation video there or at www.hillwoodmuseum.org to help set the stage for an enriching and entertaining experience.

An audio tour is free, with headsets and a brochure available when you purchase your tickets. This is highly recommended, as it walks you through the mansion and gardens and puts the home and its treasures into the context of the life of Marjorie Merriweather Post. By the time you finish, you will be in awe of both the woman and her world.

Notable Russian items include two imperial Easter eggs created by Faberge, the Orlov service commissioned by Catherine the Great for one of her many lovers and the nuptial crown of Empress Alexandra.

The vestments, chalice covers and altar cloths that the Russian government sold to finance its industrialization are tastefully displayed in the **Russian Liturgical Room**. It's sobering to pause and think about the era that followed, both for Russia and the world.

The dining table is dressed with Point de Venise lace and drips with elegance.

The decorative arts of 18th century France provided an elegant backdrop for Post's everyday life, and today they give us insight about this forward-thinking woman. Not to be missed are the two sets of drawers made by the official cabinet maker to Louis XVI and Marie Antoinette, found in the entry hall.

The transition to Hillwood's kitchen and pantry is almost startling. Post's staff enjoyed a state of the art American kitchen, complete with dumbwaiter and industrial-strength appliances – oversized meat slicers, percolators, stand mixers, double sinks and miles and miles of countertop. The Sta-Kold freezer hints that Post may have enjoyed the Birdseye vegetables that her company sold.

Pockets of beauty are everywhere, enhanced by cuttings from the gardens, and floral arrangements lead you to outdoor living spaces that are as elegant as their indoor counterparts.

The **French Parterre** transports the day tripper back to 18th century France, with its formality, symmetry, geometry and whimsical statuary. The **Rose Garden** was adapted for Post's taste by Perry Wheeler, who also assisted with the design of the Rose Garden at the White House.

A portrait of Marjorie Merriweather Post presides over the English-style library.

In the **Japanese-style Garden**, a network of paths and bridges winds past lily-padded ponds, and gardens are decorated with stone tortoises, lanterns and numerous figures. Think: Zen-like tranquility.

A Russian summer house is tucked in the woods and now used as a venue for special events. Educational programs and special exhibits are featured in the **Adirondack House**, frequently on the topic of the history of fashion.

The Russian Porcelain Room contains dinnerware that was crafted by the Imperial Porcelain Factory in St. Petersburg during the rule of the Romanovs.

Enjoying a picnic in one of the designated areas will give you a chance to savor the beauty that is Hillwood, an oasis in the city. Marjorie Merriweather Post's gift may have been extravagant, but it is also peaceful and inviting.

Of her extraordinary endeavor, Post explained, "When I began [collecting], I did it for the joy of it, and it was only as the collection grew and such interest was evidenced by others, that I came to the realization that the collection should belong to the country."

The former home of Marjorie Merriweather Post offers beauty, inspiration elegance and escapism, just minutes from the heart of Washington, DC. Thank you, Mrs. Post!

FYI:

- Hillwood is open daily, as well as some evenings and Sundays.
- Lunch is available at the Hillwood Café and the Café Express.
- Picnics are welcome in designated areas, with blankets from the Café.
- Wheelchairs and Baby Bjorns are also available for use.
- Tickets may also be purchased in the Visitors Center and online.
- Weekends are busy at Hillwood; reservations are recommended.
- Hillwood is closed in January for cleaning and renovations.
- Visit www.hillwoodmuseum.org for additional information.

The soaring design of the National Museum of the Marine Corps is a lasting tribute to the US Marines.

National Museum of the Marine Corps: Ooh-rah!

On November 11, 2006 the National Museum of the Marine Corps was established near Quantico, Virginia to honor the commitment, accomplishment and sacrifice of the US Marines. Learn about the over 200 years of dedication, honor and courage of our soldiers who are the first to fight for right and freedom.

The building itself evokes an elegant sense of pride, with its signature 210-foot stainless steel spire modeled after the raising of the flag over Iwo Jima. This iconic silhouette, beckoning travelers along I-95, has been recognized as an architectural treasure since its addition to our skyline several years ago.

An AV-8B-Harrier jump jet is suspended over the *Leatherneck gallery*, along with two Corsair fighters from WWII and a Curtiss Jenny from the 1920s.

In *Assault by Air* a Sikorsky HRS-2 helicopter disembarks a machine gun unit recreating a mission from the Korean War.

Inside, state-of-the-art multimedia technology lends amazing realism to life-size wax figures in dioramas illustrating American history through the eyes of the Marines. And you are right there with them.

Assault from the Sky depicts steely-eyed warriors jumping out of a Sikorsky helicopter and into the main rotunda. Suddenly we're transported back to Korea, and the year is 1950. Here we witness the technique of vertical envelopment, a Marine innovation still in use today, and only the glass ceiling overhead threatens to break the spell.

Not so inside the museum's galleries, leading us from the inception of the Marines in 1775 to the present day. In several instances the visitor is directly deposited into a major US conflict, and the lack of anchors to our current time and place is both breathtaking and jarring.

On the Toktong Pass near Chosin Reservoir we join the Marines – literally – while they prepare for attack by advancing Chinese soldiers. They're weary, dangerously short on ammunition and frozen to the bone, and we share a blast of cold air with them.

Surrounded and outnumbered, troops nicknamed the Frozen Chosin successfully broke free and inflicted crippling losses on the Chinese. It's no small wonder that the safest place in Korea was deemed to be "right behind a platoon of Marines" by US Army Major General Frank E. Lowe, who added, "Lord, how they could fight."

In the *Vietnam War* gallery, step through a helicopter that's been cutaway and transformed into a gateway to Hill 881, and listen to the pilot communicating with Marines on the ground. Emerge to a blast of jungle air and the sounds of combat. The deft combination of a detailed mural, sound effects and equipment brings the perilous scene to life.

The collective psyche of the Marines is explored in a brief documentary shown in the Scuttlebutt Theater. Here we learn about the spirit, heritage and responsibility that make the Marines unique, with shared traditions going back to Tun Tavern. A strong sense of sacrifice is revealed through their many voices, which describe a team where, "Uncommon valor is a common virtue."

Young visitors to the museum will enjoy a rifle range with laser simulator that lets you test your skills for $5 and try to earn an exclusive challenge coin. The day's high scores are usually posted, and many times they've been attained by Marines.

Visitors are transported into a hot landing zone via CH-46 helicopter in the *Vietnam War* gallery.

The final exhibit depicts the country's ongoing war on terrorism. Featured are a fragment from the Pentagon in Arlington and an I-beam from the World Trade Center in New York City.

The designers and architects behind this world-class museum have captured the essence of faraway times and places with authenticity and dignity, avoiding the pitfalls of sensationalism and high drama. To accomplish this, they surveyed trenches in Germany, trudged through wheat fields in France, crawled through tunnels in Japan and spent a fair amount of time in boot camp and on sea.

As a result of their thoughtful approach and accurate interpretation, the museum captures the historic events of our nation's conflicts while conveying the resolve, spirit and discipline of the US Marine Corps.

FYI:

- Admission and parking are free, and donations are accepted.
- The museum is open every day except Christmas.
- Allow at least three hours to enjoy all of the museum's galleries.
- The store features souvenirs, field rations, ornaments and gifts.
- The 200,000-square-foot facility is situated on 134 acres.
- Grounds include a picnic area, playground, walkway and chapel.

For a Square Meal – Marine style – the museum offers two dining venues – **Tun Tavern** and the **Mess Hall**.

November 10, 1775 is widely recognized as the day the US Marine Corps was born in Philadelphia's original Tun Tavern, and so the museum's very own Tun Tavern seeks to capture the look and feel of a Colonial brew house. Large paintings depicting famous Marines are displayed on the walls, and meals are reminiscent of food from the era.

The bill of fare includes modern amenities such as soups, salads and sandwiches, as well as hearty dishes like roasted turkey with pan gravy and open-face roast beef. Apple dumplings, bread pudding and chocolate brownies with ice cream ensure that nobody goes home hungry. A children's menu is available, and Tun Tavern is open daily.

Visit the Mess Hall to dine cafeteria style on homemade soup, pizza and chili, in addition to grab-and-go items and sandwiches. The Mess Hall is open daily and also welcomes children.

The museum's Tun Tavern captures the warmth of the original and features food inspired by the Colonial era.

An antique coffee grinder greets guests at the entrance to
Central Coffee Roasters in Sperryville, Virginia.

Sperryville: They've got it made in the mountains

Rappahannock County, in the foothills of the Blue Ridge Mountains, is home to some of the most talented artisans in Virginia. In the shadow of Old Rag they hone their skills, crafting small batches of single malt whiskey and creating the unique glassware to savor it in.

The first stop of the day is at **Central Coffee Roasters** (11836 Lee Highway), because we all need a little coffee to get started in the morning. Margaret Rogers and her family are living their dream, roasting small batches of beans from the furthest reaches of the world while each pursuing artistic endeavors.

Maggie's vocation is printmaking, while her husband is a carpenter and their sons rock with a bluegrass beat. Together this family brings coffee to an art form, as well.

Decide for yourself with a sample or a full-sized cup o' what I hesitate to call Joe. It's just too good. Freshly roasted light, medium and full bodied coffees from Central and South America and the East Indies are available by the pound, and blends and decaf are also offered. Freshly made granola and trail mix are also available.

The property backs up to the Thornton River, and guests are welcome to wander outside and enjoy Maggie's flower gardens.

Glassworks Gallery (11774 Lee Highway) is a visual treat. First of all, any place with a bright red suspension bridge is wicked cool. After you cross over the bridge – sans trolls peering out from underneath – colorful orbs and bowls can be seen in the gardens that line the path. The best is yet to come: Step inside and into the world of glassblower Eric Kvarnes.

The suspension bridge at Glassworks is, in itself, a work of art.

In addition to glass bowls, vessels and jewelry by Kvarnes, the gallery features unique pottery, woodwork, metalwork, photography, poetry and stained glass by the artists of Oldway Art Center, the working community of artisans that he founded.

Glassworks Gallery offers glassblowing classes to budding artists who are over 18 years of age, but you need not make a huge investment of time or money. The artist's philosophy is to let people work on a piece or two and enjoy themselves without concern about a big commitment. His motto: Life's short. Do something unusual!

The artful display of quilts on the front porch drew me into **Beech Spring Gift Shop** (11600 Lee Highway), and then I learned that one of Northern Virginia's largest quilt outlets is so much more than that.

This family-owned business has been around for four generations – selling baskets, stained glass, Polish pottery, jewelry, jams, jellies, apple butter and local fruit in season. And, of course, quilts. Best of all, this fabric art is made locally by Virginia artisans.

The Copper Fox Distillery (9 River Lane) is found behind an unassuming exterior in Sperryville's River District, off the beaten path but well worth the search. Here Rick Wasmund is cooking up American single malt whiskey and pot-stilling it, one barrel at a time.

A tour of the works gives you a peek at the distillery and inside Rick's brain. You'll follow tales of his adventures – from the inspiration to produce a fruitwood flavored whiskey, through his internship in Scotland, and up to his production of a national award winner.

In 2009 the Beverage Testing Institute awarded Wasmund's Single Malt a Gold Medal, describing it as having "bright copper color ... bold aromas of new suede, saddle soap, crème brulee and toasted banana nut bread," and a "dryish medium-full body with orange marmalade, dried apricot and sweet brown spices."

Intrigued? You can buy Wasmund's spirited products at the local ABC and in the company store. Open every day except Sunday, the shop also sells an adorable little barrel that includes the clear spirits you'll need to age a whiskey that's uniquely your own.

Rick Wasmund's product is an American single malt whiskey.

Tours are given on a limited basis throughout the week and on-the-hour on Fridays and Saturdays. If the distillery isn't in production mode at the time of your visit, you can still get a very good idea of how small batch whiskey is made. The scent of the last batch lingers for months.

Hop next door for an espresso or latte in the stylishly renovated barn dubbed Rappahannock Central. The relaxed setting of **Café Indigo** (3 River Lane) combines cottage-fresh furniture, local artwork and corrugated steel in a charming 1930s fruit-packing house.

Sharing Rappahannock Central with Café Indigo is food for the soul in the inspired galleries of **River District Arts**. This is a collective of over a dozen artists who enjoy working on site, creating while chatting with passersby. The setting bears more than a passing resemblance to Alexandria's Torpedo Factory, except this venue's found in the tranquil Shenandoah Valley. **Middle Street Gallery** features the work of member artists each month, and the **Artisan Market** offers one-of-a-kind fine Virginia crafts.

Each piece of Polish pottery at the Beech Spring Gift Shop is a bit of functional, handmade artwork.

Explore Sperryville's quaint downtown area, with restaurants and shops that sell everything from fine yarn to pottery. Antique stores are also found throughout Rappahannock County, making Sperryville the perfect day trip if you'd like to infuse a little warmth into your home.

Or, if you just like fine whiskey and good coffee.

Shops and restaurants line Main Street, providing a scenic stroll before the drive home.

FYI:

- This trip is best on a Saturday during the spring, summer or fall.
- Central Coffee Roasters is open Fridays, Saturdays and Sundays.
- The Glassworks Gallery is open every day but Wednesdays.
- Beech Spring Gift Shop is open most days.
- The Copper Fox Distillery is closed on Sundays.
- River District Arts is open on weekends.

The National Museum of Crime and Punishment is located in a stylishly
renovated building in DC's Penn Quarter.

Elaine C. Jean

National Museum of Crime and Punishment: Busted!

The National Museum of Crime and Punishment in Washington, DC boasts over 25,000 square feet of murder, mayhem and misdemeanor. And while they like to claim that a visit is "so much fun, it's a crime," their emphasis on retribution underscores the point that this is no laughing matter.

The cat-and-mouse dance of law enforcer and evil doer is a prevalent theme in the five distinct galleries of the **National Museum of Crime and Punishment** (575 7th Street NW) each delving into the study of criminal intent, criminal profiling, the penal system and more. Where else can you gaze into the mind of a serial killer?

The museum houses the vintage car used in the 1967 movie *Bonnie and Clyde,* which stared Warren Beatty and Fay Dunaway.

Ted Bundy's '68 Volkswagen greets you in the lobby, where you can see the diabolically redesigned vehicle he lured victims to and unwittingly left vital forensic evidence in. You'll have barely touched the tip of the iceberg, but you'll be hooked.

The evolution of crime and punishment throughout history is explored, beginning with inhumane devices of the Middle Ages. An exhibit on America's first criminals illustrates how the moral and upstanding folk of Colonial America meted out retribution for the heinous crime of kissing the wife on Sabbath.

As the country grew westward the true outlaw was born, followed by the cold-blooded bank robber of the Great Depression. One highlight of the museum is the Bonnie and Clyde car, a replica of their 1934 Ford, complete with 167 authentically placed bullet holes.

When America got all mobbed up Al Capone became its most notorious criminal, and his luxurious cell from Eastern State Penitentiary is recreated in vivid detail. In addition, prison culture is illustrated with an inmate art gallery, a nifty collection of shivs and an entire wall devoted to tattoos.

An exhibit about Capone's incarceration hints that he may have still wielded power at Eastern State Penitentiary, but not at Alcatraz.

The museum's patrol car simulator is the same as those used by police academies to train officers.

Arguably the most chilling artifact of all is Tennessee's venerable Old Smokey, the workhorse that administered countless volts of justice to 125 inmates. A stainless steel gas chamber is modern by comparison and eerie with sound effects.

Armchair detectives will love the interactive nature of this museum. A patrol car simulator puts you in the driver's seat to pursue a perp through city streets, and the firearms training scenario has you busting a meth house and making the kill shot.

The museum's crime lab explains the science of analyzing footprints, fingerprints and ballistics, and now offers a Unabomber exhibit featuring Ted Kaczynski's personal belongings. But the star of this gallery is its cadaver, on an interactive autopsy table. Yes, seriously.

The **America's Most Wanted** stage is found in the basement and serves as home to occasional broadcasts of the show that is responsible for the apprehension of over 1,000 criminals.

While the National Museum of Crime and Punishment's displays are state-of-the-art and glitzy, they avoid glamorizing a life of crime.

Everyday heroes from local police officers and forensic specialists to FBI agents and profilers are the real stars of this show.

Next explore the neighborhood of **Penn Quarter**: Where there's plenty to eat and a Starbucks on every block. The stretch of 7th Street between Chinatown and Pennsylvania Avenue has undergone revitalization, transforming it into a destination for food lovers and sightseers alike.

The vibrant community includes the Warner, National, Shakespeare, Wooly Mammoth and Ford's Theaters, as well as numerous museums. Spectators flock to the Verizon Center for Washington Wizards and Capitals games, and all those hungry fans need food.

Legal Seafood (704 7th Street NW) will put you on the right side of the law after a day at the museum. This is the place to grab a cup of chowder, a lobster roll and a microbrew. An all-day menu features portions that are easy on the wallet and waistline.

Carmine's (425 7th Street NW) serves their meals family style, so bring your appetite and some of the usual suspects to share Italian-American favorites from New York – lasagna, chicken parm and shrimp scampi. The five-liter bottle of Sangiovese is also meant for sharing – with 14 of your closest friends.

Jaleo (480 7th Street NW) is known for having introduced tapas – Spain's traditional small plates that are big on flavor – to the area. Authentic paellas, grilled meats and cheese plates are featured, along with seafood and veggie offerings. Sangria and sherries are featured.

District Chop House and Brewery (509 7th Street NW) is unabashedly masculine and known for steakhouse classics paired with handcrafted ales that are brewed onsite. Weekend brunch offers the Chophouse spin on breakfast classics.

Clyde's at Gallery Place (707 7th Street NW) also serves brunch in a setting that blends the Victorian era with Asian influences. The menu includes Clyde's famous crab cakes and seasonal specials, as well as favorites from their other locations in the Metro area.

Red Velvet Cupcakery (501 7th Street NW) has added Hazelnut Café and gluten-free White Velvet cupcakes to a line-up of classics that include Devil's Food and Carrot Cake. This is the best place to grab a portable bit of comfort food.

Pitango Gelato (413 7th Street NW) combines traditional methods with simple, premium ingredients to produce gelato and sorbet that's big on flavor but lower in fat than ice cream. They also make a mean cup of coffee.

There are several parking garages in the area, and once you've parked the car you can hoof it for the remainder of the day. On-street, metered parking is free on Sundays and plentiful when you arrive at Penn Quarter by 9:30 a.m., before the opening of the museum. If you use the Metro, the closest stop is Gallery Place/Chinatown.

FYI:

- The museum is open daily but closed on Thanksgiving Day.
- Admission is reasonable, with discounts for children.
- Tickets are sold online at www.crimemuseum.com.
- Special discount rates apply for seniors, military, retired military, police and retired police.

Carpe Weekend's tip:

Parkmobile allows you to pay for parking without digging in your pockets for stray coins. Use spaces marked with their green sign and pay via downloaded app with your smart phone. To learn more, visit us.parkmobile.com.

The International Spy Museum is located at 800 F Street NW, in the historic
LeDroit Building.
Courtesy of the International Spy Museum

International Spy Museum: From DC with love

The District of Columbia is home to more spies than any other city on Earth, so it should come as no surprise that the city plays host to the museum that features the most artifacts of international espionage, trickery and intrigue.

The **International Spy Museum** (800 F Street NW), located in the Penn Quarter, offers visitors an opportunity to trace the evolution of spying throughout history with audiovisual displays, interactive exhibits and role playing. The stylish 20,000-square-foot building may be big on glitz and glamour, but it makes every attempt to give an accurate look behind the scenes of an industry that's typically cloaked in secrecy.

An orientation film in the briefing room describes techniques and tools of the trade, as well as insight on the motivation for making this career choice. Visitors separate fact from fiction, dismissing common misconceptions as the real world of espionage comes into focus.

Ever want to work under cover? Break a code? Sniff out the spies among us? It's all in a day's work at the International Spy Museum. The first order of business is to choose a new identity from among 16 profiles and memorize the details as if your life depended on it. In the everyday life of a spy, it would.

If you don't have a lot of experience in the practice of deception, the *Tricks of the Trade* gallery is a veritable school for spies. This exhibit explains how agents are recruited and trained and shows the nifty gadgets they've used – dubbed tradecraft – to carry out their missions.

Secret cameras, hidden listening devices and clandestine concealment containers are featured, with the doggie doo safe eliciting giggles from the younger set. The fine art of disguise is described, with hints on how you, too, can do this at home with the squint of an eye or the furrow of a brow. Ingenuity is crucial to survival in the life of a spy.

Kids can crawl through overhead ductwork and hear recordings of private conversations among aids to Fidel Castro – a sobering reminder that you're not backstage at *Get Smart*, and this is not a game. Because America does, however, love a good spy flick, you will see several exhibits devoted to the genre.

And who best personifies our obsession with the bullet-dodging spy? Bond. James Bond. The museum's Aston Martin DB5, used to promote the 1964 movie *Goldfinger,* draws in viewers with its sexy lines and promises of escape.

Bond author Ian Fleming is highlighted in *The Secret History of History,* a gallery that reveals the role that intelligence has played in shaping world events. Fleming knew of which he wrote, having been a British Navy intelligence officer with a penchant for fast cars, fast women and games of chance.

America's first president was also its first spymaster, and it is fascinating to learn how George Washington built an intelligence network and passed along disinformation to the Redcoats. When the Revolutionary War was over, Britain's master of espionage in America complained that, "Washington did not really outfight the British, he simply outspied us!"

Displays about the famous Mata Hari, exotic dancer turned WWI spy, as well as Josephine Baker and Julia Child, remind the visitor that espionage is not an all-boys club. Women spies were so prevalent during WWII that propaganda posters warned men to avoid pillow talk.

The museum's collection of cryptology equipment is understandably extensive. *Breaking the Code* includes a Jeffersonian cipher device, a message scrambler used by the Confederate army, and the infamous German cipher machine from WWII. Interactive activities and exhibits allow you to try your hand at code breaking.

Perhaps the most impressive gallery in the International Spy Museum is *Behind Enemy Lines*, devoted to the Cold War. Since Berlin was the capital of the Cold War, it makes an appropriate backdrop for exhibits on the topic. And its city café – complete with tables and chairs – is the place to temporarily recover from sensory overload. A replica of the tunnel beneath the border of the American and Soviet sectors of Berlin further lends a feeling of authenticity.

The Wilderness of Mirrors, featuring real-life spies of the late 20th century – Aldrich Ames, John Walker, Anthony Blunt and Robert Philip Hanssen – is a look at cases that dominated our headlines not that long ago. The 12-minute film *Cat and Mouse* is worth watching for its insight on the apprehension of both Ames and Hanssen by the agents who were hot on their trails.

The tour ends with the *Weapons of Mass Disruption* gallery, and the final film, *Ground Truth*, warns of the challenges facing intelligence professionals in their mission to protect our county and its infrastructure in the Digital Age.

The 5,000 –square-foot store offers an amazing selection of souvenirs, including recording devices, spy apparel, code kits, invisible ink pens and concealment devices, as well as the usual tee shirts, key chains and postcards. Hands down, this is one of the best museum gift shops in DC.

FYI:

- The museum is open daily but closed on major holidays.
- Hours vary by season.
- Reasonably priced tickets may be purchased online or at the museum.
- The building is wheelchair accessible.
- Strollers, food, drinks and photography are not allowed.
- The nearest Metro station is Gallery Place/Chinatown.
- Visit www.spymuseum.org for hours and other information.
- The Spy City Café serves breakfast, lunch and dinner. Zola is also in the building.

The Calvary Battles of Aldie, Middleburg and Upperville by Robert F.
O'Neil Jr. was commissioned by Paul Mellon as a tribute to the more than
1 million horses killed or wounded during the Civil War.

Middleburg: Horse-centric hometown America

*Virginia's capital of horses, hounds and fox hunting, Middleburg is
sometimes dismissed as a genteel playground for the rich and famous.
But with fine restaurants, eclectic boutiques and a museum dedicated to
the sporting arts – all set against a charming and historic backdrop –
who's to say this little village can't be your playground, too?*

For some, the topic of equestrian and field art conjures up images of
steeplechase races and pedigreed pets. But the **National Sporting
Library and Museum** (102 The Plains Road) goes well beyond the
expected by illustrating how our country's contributions to the genre
have evolved, developing a distinct style that's rooted in the wild place
that America once was.

Here we are made witness to the visceral dance of predator versus prey,
whether viewing a painting of a man and his son bonding while bagging
dinner or of a fox pursuing a solitary meal in the freshly fallen snow. The
relatively new museum deftly reveals that it would be a mistake to
cubbyhole sporting art as the territory of the aristocratic.

The setting – in a renovated and expanded 1804 property in the middle of
Hunt Country – serves to enhance its presentations of the art, literature
and culture of our equestrian, hunting and fishing endeavors. Exhibitions
change regularly and succeed in portraying the thrill of the hunt, with the
anticipation – and terror – it so often entails. This, folks, is high drama.

Curator Claudia Pfeiffer maintains an overarching theme of the
preservation of our open space. She lends broad appeal to thought-
provoking exhibitions by taking an evolutionary approach, reflecting the
diversity of America's lifestyles, wildlife and landscape. A visit is as
much a lively study of history and culture as it is a study of art.

Foxhounds and Terrier in a Stable Interior by John Emms is part of the
permanent collection and was a gift from Felicia Warburg Rogan.
Courtesy of the National Sporting Library and Museum

An interactive approach makes the museum user-friendly and accessible.
Monthly sketching events invite budding artists of all ages to visit on
select Sundays with their drawing materials, working alongside local
talent in a comfortable and informal setting.

Next door is the **National Sporting Library**, founded in 1954 and
housing over 24,000 books in a facility that's open to researchers and to
the general public. Perched on a hill in historic and horsey Middleburg,
the Vine Hill campus is an architectural statement that the equestrian and
field sports are alive and well and living in Loudoun County.

A collection of American weathervanes donated by the late Paul Mellon
in 1999 is sprinkled throughout the library, revealing the whimsical side
of country life. Inscribed silver trophies await their next equestrian
events, illustrating a deep and enduring sense of community spirit and
pride.

During regular visiting hours anyone can view artifacts in the Forrest E.
Mars Sr. Exhibit Hall and peruse the library's shelves. While materials

are not available for loan, there are plenty of alcoves with places to sit, read and conduct research. Children's books make this a welcoming stop for horse lovers and sporting enthusiasts of all ages.

A tour of the F. Ambrose Clark Rare Book Room is available to the public by reservation only. The rare books collection includes an autographed manuscript on foxhunting by Theodore Roosevelt and 90 editions of Izaak Walton's *The Compleat Angler*, as well as original copies of *Audubon Magazine*.

Several weathervanes donated by Paul Mellon are on display in the National Sporting Library.
Courtesy of the National Sporting Library and Museum

The town of Middleburg is Loudoun County's alternative to the shopping mall. With upscale shops, fine restaurants, fun bakeries and over a dozen antique stores, you can easily spend a few hours soaking in the unique flavor of the town and shopping for the people you care about. You'll never have to resort to the Jelly of the Month Club again.

Antique shops specialize in everything from watches to firearms for the collector on your list. And for the romantic, the **Middleburg Antique Emporium** (107 W. Washington Street) sells one-of-a-kind items in a setting that exudes charm. This is the place to buy a bit of tony old Middleburg to bring home with you.

The Fun Shop (117 W. Washington Street) offers soaps, linens, beeswax candles, jewelry and pottery, as well as a collection of delightfully tacky ties. Shop here for horsey souvenirs of the day – ornaments, nightlights, coffee cups and puzzles – and a great assortment of wine chillers, baskets, paper goods, linens and cocktail hardware to set the proper tablescape for a Twilight Polo picnic at Great Meadows. Heck, they'll even sell you one of those classy little folding tables.

The **Christmas Sleigh** (5 E. Washington Street) is packed with European decorations and nutcrackers depicting the not-so-usual suspects – Ulysses S. Grant, Robert E. Lee, William Shakespeare and Yoda – in addition to a collection of traditional German and Austrian clothing in the back. They have all your lederhosen needs covered in a most tasteful way. A glass case packed with equestrian-themed items – silver tea sets, foxy napkin rings and a candelabras – will have you looking forward to your next formal tailgating affair.

Middleburg offers a café or bakery on nearly every block, making it easy to grab a couple of cookies and coffee to fuel the shopping as you go. **The Upper Crust** (2 N. Pendleton Street) is a local favorite for its cookies, cakes and pies, but they're especially known for their cow puddles. The shop sells sandwiches and lunch items, as do several cafes in town.

Market Salamander (200 W. Washington Street) is a working chef's market that produces a farm country breakfast, fruit, scones and some of the best sandwiches in town, as well as dinner-to-go. Heavier fare leans to gourmet comfort food and includes meatloaf, fried chicken and mac and cheese. Take-out picnics include light offerings and may be ordered in advance and picked up before 7 p.m. – in time for evening events.

Fancier food is found at a handful of venerable dining establishments. **The French Hound** (101 S. Madison Street) is tucked away on a back road and offers lunch and dinner several days a week in a Federal-style house with sunny Provencal décor. A meal here is like a quick romp to France – only everyone speaks English and the food is not the least bit off-putting. Pumpkin profiteroles marry French cooking with the best of the Virginia countryside, and they shouldn't be missed.

The Fox's Den (7 W. Washington Street) is tucked in the basement of one of the oldest structures in Middleburg. Dating back to the late 1700s, the building is rumored to have hidden John Mosby's horse while the Confederate colonel used Middleburg as his base camp. While the restaurant has retained its interior stone walls and rich historic atmosphere, its menu is upscale yet casual and includes favorites such as wild mushroom risotto, garlicky mussels and fresh salads, as well as big burgers and juicy steaks. Fireside dining makes for a romantic evening.

The Red Fox Inn and Tavern captures the equestrian spirit and charm of Middleburg.

A trip to Middleburg wouldn't be complete without a visit to the **Red Fox Inn and Tavern** (2 E. Washington Street). Established in 1728 as Chinn's Ordinary, the Red Fox offers hearty lunch and dinner selections in a setting that's steeped in history. Hand-hewn ceiling beams and a blazing fireplace embody that unmistakable Middleburg look and feel. As you enjoy crab cakes, rainbow trout and grilled duck breast, consider that past diners have included John Kennedy, Pamela Harriman, Jacqueline Kennedy Onassis, Elizabeth Taylor and Senator John Warner.

Middleburg is an easy day trip from Washington, DC, just an hour by car. But if you really want to connect with Hunt Country, you'll stay overnight at the **Middleburg Country Inn** (209 E. Washington Street). Walking distance from it all, the inn offers an elegant, relaxed way of life that will have you scheming to make it your own.

Eight rooms suit a variety of tastes and include rich regional décor, private baths, wireless internet, luxurious bedding and full made-to-order breakfasts. Innkeepers Jo Ann and Kevin Hazard extend heart-warming hospitality with kind words and spot-on restaurant recommendations and reservations. Freshly baked cookies, glasses of wine and scoops of ice cream will make you feel right at home, whether you're out on the deck, in the parlor or in your own comfy room.

The Middleburg County Inn offers luxurious accommodations in an updated and tasteful historic setting.

A bed and breakfast inn is only as good as its morning repast, and so the eggs benedict, old-style waffles, country breakfast and hot maple oats – served in a lovely breakfast room that's open to guests of the inn only – define this as one of the best. Seasonal fruit and lemon cake made from a family recipe round out the menu.

Jo Ann recommends heading south to **The Plains** for a change of pace and a whole 'nother village to explore. **Crest Hill Antiques and Tea Room** (4303 Fauquier Avenue) is open from Wednesday through Sunday and offers tea room fare in a charming country setting that features vintage furnishings, accessories, fine gifts, jewelry and books. This stop, alone, is worth the detour.

Fashioned after tea shops found in small villages of the English countryside, Crest Hill serves over 25 varieties of tea, along with coffee, hot cocoa, apple cider and lemonade. Pastries, cakes, scones, cookies and tea bread are good at any time of day, and tea sandwiches, fruit platters, hearty soups and fresh salads provide substantial lunches. Themed "special-teas" include Tea for Two and the Full Monty.

The Plains boasts several highly regarded restaurants and eclectic shops selling everything from home furnishings and antiques to artwork and fine crafts.

The Whole Ox (6364 Stuart Street) bills itself as the neighborhood butcher shop in the middle of nowhere. Their inspired array of beef, lamb, poultry, fish, cheeses, charcuterie and other randomly delicious stuff makes the middle of nowhere look like somewhere special.

FYI:

- This trip is best made during weekends from May – September.
- The museum is open daily except on Mondays and federal holidays.
- Admission is free; to enhance your experience, visit www.nsl.org.
- The NSLM holds events, open houses and a book fair each year.
- For details about shops and restaurants, visit individual websites.
- To learn more about The Plains, visit www.ThePlainsVirginia.com.

Carpe Weekend's tip:

The Middleburg area hosts numerous events throughout the year. For exact dates and details, visit www.greatmeadow.org and www.middleburg.org.

May	Hunt Country Stable Tour/Saturday Twilight Polo begins
June	Upperville Colt and Horse Show
July	July 4th at Great Meadows
Aug.	Middleburg Annual Sidewalk Sale
Sept.	Saturday Twilight Polo concludes
Oct.	International Gold Cup at Great Meadows
Nov.	Middleburg Christmas Shop at Emmanuel Episcopal Church
Dec.	Middleburg Hunt Parade and Christmas in Middleburg

The staff of Sweet Angelina's Cupcakery takes its work seriously, with dreams of entering the Food Network's *Cupcake Wars*.

7. A SEASON FOR EVERY REASON

Winter in Frederick: Feather your nest

The British poet Dame Edith Sitwell declared, "Winter is the time for comfort, for good food and warmth, for the touch of a good friend's hand and for a talk beside the fire. It is the time for home." A trip to Frederick, Maryland can help turn your house into a place Dame Edith would happily hibernate in.

Founded in 1745 by German and English settlers, the historic town has long been recognized as a go-to place for antique furnishings. The Clintons were said to stop and shop here on their way to the presidential retreat at Camp David, so you never who you might rub elbows with.

First, drive to the **Frederick Visitors Center** (151 S. East Street) for a bit of local history. The center is housed in a beautifully restored, circa 1899 warehouse that sets the stage for the day. It offers convenient hours, off-street parking, free maps and a brief film about attractions and upcoming events in Frederick.

Next, travel along East Street and the area known as **Everedy Square and Shab Row**. This cluster of restored 19th century buildings now offers dining, entertainment and plenty of shopping, with free, untimed parking in the back. You can leave your car here and travel on foot for the rest of the day.

The Loft at Antique Imports layers old with new, blending antiques with Design Center goodies.

The **Loft at Antique Imports** (125 N. East Street) is the starting point of our tour – with its urban-chic blend of old and new – artfully housed in a renovated cigar factory. Gorgeous antiques meet DC Design Center samples, with a generous sprinkling of handmade items. This is a place for the decoratively challenged to gather ideas, and for the savvy shopper to pick up that special accent piece and nab a bargain on high-end upholstered furniture.

The **Little Pottery Shop** (117 N. East Street) offers pottery ranging from casual to elegant, so there's something to compliment any décor. Each piece has been made by hand, and most are functional as well as decorative. This is art you can both use and admire.

A large concentration of stores selling antiques and the decorative arts is found on Patrick Street, an easy walk to the southeast, so consult your map and head downtown.

Detour to **Great Stuff by Paul** (10 N. Carroll Street), where you'll often find antiques for the home and garden put to surprising new uses. Past visits have yielded a Dutch clog doing double duty as a planter and a sugar mold stand repurposed as a candle holder. Paul's other building at 257 E. 6th Street is touted as a world in a warehouse, with unique items from China and Europe.

Back on the main drag, over a dozen shops transform a few city blocks into one-stop shopping for home decorators.

Emporium Antiques (112 E. Patrick Street) is a long-time favorite, housing a maze of shops run by over 100 vendors selling everything from cut crystal to heavy furniture. Stop by for the quilts, lace, antique toys, vintage jewelry and mink coats destined to dress up your life, as well as the farm tables, deacon benches and grandfather clocks to add substance.

Emporium Antiques has just about everything you'd expect at an antique store, except the dust.

For another dose of inspiration, visit the **Dream House** (102 E. Patrick Street), where furnishings and accessories are arranged in a way that both dazzles and empowers. If you don't have the time or the inclination to pull it all together for yourself, they offer a full range of design services.

Pieces at the Little Pottery Shop are thrown and shaped by hand.

It's the little things that transform a house – kitchen, bar, baby and pet items, as well as frames and seasonal touches – and that's what's featured at **Home Essentials of Frederick** (38 E. Patrick Street). Don't miss the wall of Memory Blocks by Sid Dickens, a Vancouver-based artist who adorns individual hand cast plaster tiles with meaningful themes of historic, romantic and religious significance.

Silk and Burlap (28 E. Patrick Street) creates a world that is that is both cottage-fresh and sophisticated. Rustic tables, vintage glassware and new table linens are presented by two owners who have extensive experience in retail and an eye for detail. Theirs is a lifestyle shop with an ever-changing inventory, so it pays to visit often to see what's new. Relish Décor also offers design services from this location.

The new kid on the block is **Salvaged**, just across the street (29 E. Patrick Street). As the daughter of Tennessee antique dealers, this shop's owner has an affinity for varnish and a love of history in her blood. The store offers intriguing pieces that have been acquired at auctions, estate sales and barns. Some have been refinished, and many are accompanied by written stories. Decorative accessories are new and made by hand and in the United States whenever possible.

Frederick also has several consignment stores, such as **Fabulous Finds** (24 E. Patrick Street) and **Heritage Antiques** (39 E. Patrick Street), both selling antiques and gently used furnishings that keep a modest budget in check.

The town features a growing number of good restaurants, many found on nearby Market Street. But chances are you'll be too busy to sit down and eat, and that's where the local cupcakeries come into play.

Back at Everedy Square and Shab Row, you can sample the diminutive desserts of both **Sweet Angela's Cupcakery** (244 E. Church Street) and **angelcakes** (319 E. Church Street). Each offers perennial favorites, as well as daily specials that combine fun flavors with creative flair. At less than $3 each, you can afford to decide who wins Frederick's duel of diminutive desserts for yourself.

FYI:

- This trip is best made on weekends year round.
- Check individual websites for days and hours of operation.
- For a map and additional information, visit www.fredericktourism.org.

Carpe Weekend's tip:

More than 80 shops, galleries and restaurants are open until 9 p.m. on First Saturday, with free events and activities. Past celebrations have included ice sculptures at *Fire in Ice* in February and puppy love at *Dog Days of Summer* in September. Visit www.downtownfrederick.org for upcoming first Saturday of the month themes.

Shumba brings a happy vibe to the corner of 7th and C Streets.

Spring at Eastern Market: Good day, sunshine

When spring is in the air, Washington, DC's Eastern Market bursts with fresh flowers and good things to eat – as well as an eclectic collection of arts, crafts and antiques. A visit to one of the nation's oldest open air markets is a nod to blue skies and sunny days ahead.

Built in 1873, **Eastern Market** (225 7th Street SE) was originally intended as a place to distribute provisions and create a sense of community on Capitol Hill. It still does both quite nicely.

A local favorite, **Market Lunch** serves the best breakfast around but never on a Sunday. So if you want to try the blueberry buckwheat pancakes – affectionately called Blue Bucks – or their colossal egg, potato, cheese and meat sandwich known simply as the Brick, arrive at South Hall early on a Saturday and prepare to be friendly.

This is a cash-only establishment, and diners cue up in a line that looks long but moves quickly. Place orders in at the counter and read the posted rules while you wait, then grab a seat at a communal table and prepare to meet your neighbors. Washington insiders rub elbows – literally – with suburbanites and tourists, and a theme of congeniality carries throughout the day.

After breakfast, be sure not to linger at the table – that's one of the rules. You won't want to when you see the collection of butchers, seafood mongers, bakers and cheese vendors that fill the adjacent **South Hall Market**. This Italianate-style pavilion was rebuilt after suffering a three-alarm fire in 2007, and now it's back, better than ever.

The Italianate brick Eastern Market draws locals and tourists year round.

The family-owned businesses that fill the market have been here for decades. **Bowers Fancy Dairy Products** has been supplying Washingtonians with their cholesterol fix for over fifty years, purveying a wide array of domestic and international cheeses as well as local dairy items. They often pass out samples so you can taste the difference that quality and freshness make.

Eastern Market is, in fact, all about quality: **Canales'** Italian Prosciutto, **Calomiris'** Greek honey and olive oil, the **Fine Sweet Shop's** Kosher baked goods and **Union Meat Company's** half smokes, knockwurst and kielbasa are just a few of the items that foodies come to hunt and gather every week.

Tables brim with produce and shoppers chat with vendors along **Farmers Line** on the weekends, when an open-air market spills out of the building. Much of the food sold here is from the rural areas of Virginia, West Virginia, Maryland, Delaware and Pennsylvania.

The 7th Street thoroughfare in front of the market is closed to vehicles on the weekends, and the resulting pedestrian mall is home to booths, tables and stalls selling a variety of handmade items – jewelry, soaps, children's clothing, sketches, watercolor paintings and other artwork.

Manatho Shumba Masani is set up at the corner of 7th and C Streets, where he's been working wire and soda containers into Canimals for several years. Shumba's cleaning up the planet one can at a time while showcasing contemporary music and Zimbabwean sculpting techniques.

The artist is fun to watch and easy to talk to, and his trademark giraffe is a favorite for its expressive face and graceful features. Who knew Arizona Iced Tea cans could look this good?

Market Pottery is located in the basement of South Hall, entered by walking around Shumba's booth and past the patriotic panels painted by his neighbor. Artisans have flocked here for over five decades, and the works of a half-dozen potters are displayed and sold in the front room.

Eastern Market features a wide array of fresh fruits and veggies.

Capitol Hill Flea Market –the area's incubator for small businesses – is now entering its 29th year. Antiques, arts and crafts inspire both casual browsers and avid shoppers alike, with offerings that go beyond the usual flea market finds.

Red Persimmon Imports offers handmade, fair trade gifts and accessories, and **Olde Good Things** brings architectural elements – stained glass, iron fencing, pressed tin and marble mantles salvaged from grand old buildings. A number of food vendors dot the landscape, selling everything from empanadas to falafel.

Nearby popular attractions include the Library of Congress and US Botanic Gardens, and restaurants line the portion of 8th Street known as Barracks Row.

The **Barrack's Row Heritage Trail** (7th Street and Pennsylvania Avenue) begins near the Eastern Market train station and takes about an hour to complete. A free guidebook, available to download at culturaltourismdc.org, will lead you through the stomping ground of John Philip Sousa.

The trail passes the **Marine Barracks** – the oldest continuously manned Marine post in the country – as well as the historic Washington Navy Yard and other points of interest. Interpretive signage brings into focus Barracks Row residents who've lived and worked here while serving their country.

Wares at the Capitol Hill Flea Market reflect the eclectic tastes of residents.

Market Pottery operates down under the market, where it has been hidden for 50 years.

FYI:

- Market Lunch doesn't serve breakfast on Sundays.
- Eastern Market is closed on Mondays.
- Eastern Market features live music most weekends.
- Special events take place year round.
- For a complete list of events, visit www.easternmarket-dc.org.

Carpe Weekend's tip:

Parking can be problematic on Capitol Hill, so using the train is recommended. If you drive and would like to park on street, visit us.parkmobile.com and download their app to feed the meter by phone.

The Bollman Iron Truss Bridge, near Savage Mill, was built by the B&O
Railroad in 1869.

Spring Break at Savage Mill: Leave the daily grind

Located on the falls of Maryland's Patuxent River near the planned community of Columbia, Historic Savage Mill is a quick drive from both Baltimore and Washington, DC. Its latest incarnation – a maze of antique stores, gift shops and restaurants – is a 21st century monument to 19th century industrial America.

Historic Savage Mill (8600 Foundry Street) is much more than a historic textile mill turned shopping venue. It's a destination that offers activities ranging from the athletic to the cerebral, with something to please every member of the family, especially during Spring Break.

Kids love the unexpected thrill of a 330-foot zip line – an outdoor attraction that changes the whole idea of a shopping trip with Mom. The historic property is also a photographer's paradise – especially in the late winter and early spring, when trees are light of foliage and likely to reveal the surrounding landscape's soul.

The mill was founded in 1820 by the Williams brothers and funded by John Savage to the tune of $20,000. Their weaving machines were originally powered by a 30-foot water wheel that harnessed the energy of the river to produce canvas for Baltimore's clipper ships, as well as for the tents, cannon covers and rucksacks of the Civil War.

Hollywood turned to the Savage Mill for textiles to paint as backdrops for turn-of-the-century silent films. When two world wars brought the need for miles and miles of canvas, the mill was enlisted to produce it. Even with the operation's eventual shutdown after World War II, the mill's story of ingenuity and reinvention didn't end.

The structure operated as a Christmas village from 1947 to 1950, and it was put on the National Register of Historic Places in 1974. Today it's a shopping complex, and buildings are named for the stages in a production process that took place there over a century ago – Carding, Spinning, Old Weave and New Weave. Each area now contains a wide array of decorative items, gifts and antiques. But at this mall, there's as much to do on the outside as there is on the inside.

If you enjoy looking back in time through a lens, dress warmly and bring a camera. Here the decaying remnants of history are as photogenic as the stylishly restored, and opportunities for both abstract views and natural images abound. Even if you're not an avid shutterbug, you may find yourself giving your smartphone a workout.

The mill's showpiece is the **Bollman Truss Bridge**, a semi-suspension masterpiece that was relocated to the property so the B & O Railroad could cross the Patuxent River and service the mill. Made of wrought and cast iron, it is the last remaining bridge of its kind. Other artifacts are found along the waterline – some yet-to-be restored – and a lack of interpretive signage lets the imagination run wild.

Kids who've tagged along for the day and are looking for something a little more exciting can check out **TagParty RECON**'s outdoor laser tag on four wildly wooded acres. And if they're craving multiple levels of fun, **Terrapin Adventures** delivers – with diversions including a zip line, giant swing, climbing tower and challenge course. Walk-ins are accepted, but reservations are recommended.

When hunger or curiosity gets the better of you, head inside and grab a map to negotiate through the marketplace of stores, boutiques, restaurants, folk art, fine art, craft galleries and dealers of antiques and collectibles. Shops offer a little bit of everything, and owners love to chat with customers about their wares.

For coffee, croissants and other French pastries, visit **Bonaparte Breads** in the Carding Building. If heavier food is in order, find the **Rams Head Tavern** – an Annapolis institution for seafood, steaks, burgers and beers.

Savage Mill offers a little bit of everything but leans toward the artsy-craftsy, with beading, stamping and scrapbooking supplies as well as yarns for knitting and fabrics for quilting. Games and toys for everyone from the kids to the family dog are found throughout the complex.

The **Antique Center** is accessed from the courtyard and is a focal point, featuring more than 200 dealers of furniture, accessories and gift items. On a recent visit, vintage glassware, Americana and homespun goodness prevailed. The Historic Savage Mill has been deemed the best place to buy antiques in Howard County by the *Baltimore Sun*.

When Spring Break is just around the corner, Historic Savage Mill provides a fun excursion and engaging diversion for every member of the family – whether historian, photographer, antique collector, crafter or daredevil. Cries of, "I'm bored" will be chased away, at least for a day.

FYI:

- Historic Savage Mill is open daily, with Sunday the best day to visit.
- Ample parking is found in the rear of the buildings.
- Jazz Brunch is offered on Sundays at the Ram's Head Tavern.
- Auctions are held Sundays and Wednesdays in the Cotton Shed; visit www.caplans.com for schedule.

Carpe Weekend's tip:

Terrapin Adventures usually offers a Spring Break special. Call (301) 725-1313 for a promo code to use while booking online. Visit www.terrapinadventures.com to find details about this and other upcoming events. Similarly, TagParty RECON posts special offers and promotions at www.tagpartyrecon.com.

The Aldie Mill offers visitors a glimpse of the past, when mills were a vital part of life in the rural South.

Summer in Loudoun County: What's it all about, Aldie?

The quaint little village of Aldie, Virginia is big on personality, radiating from eclectic shops that line its stretch of the John Mosby Highway. The antique gristmill hosts a variety of events and still serves as the centerpiece of this likeable town.

The restored **Aldie Mill** (39401 John Mosby Highway) and the architecture that grew up around it bring visitors back to an Aldie that thrived in a previous life and a different way. The mill became the hub of its community soon after it was completed by Charles Fenton Mercer in the early 19th century.

Here local grain was ground into flour and transported to Alexandria via the newly completed Little River Turnpike, then shipped up and down the East Coast and to Europe. Today demonstrations of Virginia's only surviving gristmill of its kind are held every afternoon on the weekends, from mid-April to mid-November. A visit offers a rare opportunity to see the impressive tandem overshot waterwheels in motion.

Special events are scheduled throughout the year, and in the past have included *A Spirited Tasting of History and Whiskey*, as well as the award-winning annual Aldie Harvest Festival in October.

The **Aldie Peddler** (39484 John Mosby Highway) is well known by locals as a purveyor of fine and reasonably priced wines, Amish furniture and affordable antiques. But it's the shop's owner, Wally Lunceford, that gives the place its heart and soul.

The boyishly handsome proprietor is often found here, meeting and greeting customers and making the mood a little lighter. Wally's multi-liter wine glass may be literally and figuratively half full, but he's seriously knowledgeable on the topic of wine.

The Aldie Peddler boasts a great selection of wines from Virginia, California, Chile, Austria, Australia, New Zealand, South Africa, Spain and France.

Free tastings are offered throughout the year, with tidbits of food and copious amounts of laughter. The Aldie Peddler is open every day except on Mondays.

Next-door neighbor **Bella Villa** (39478 John Mosby Highway) shares the beautiful world of Rosanna Smith, and a visit will inspire you to new decorating heights. She reports that past finds have included "glorious chandeliers straight from the canals of Venice, Italy" and "crusty mirrors that somehow make everyone look beautiful."

Rosanna clearly has a knack for marketing, as well as for collecting interesting items from around the globe, And she makes a mean cup of espresso, too. Bella Villa is open afternoons from Wednesday through Sunday, proudly features an entire room of "mantiques."

Across the street, **Mattingly's** (39469 John Mosby Highway) specializes in outdoor furniture to suit most purposes – picnic tables, swings, bars, birdhouses and enormous rocking lounge chairs that beg you to drag the big screen TV outdoors and grab a beer. These are the La-Z-Boy recliner of the Amish world. Visit Mattingly's daily from Monday through Saturday; they're closed on Sundays.

Offering china, paintings, prints, decorative items and sturdy furniture from a variety of periods, **Mercer Tavern** (39359 John Mosby Highway) is cozy and cluttered – in a good way.

Mary Ann and Tucker Withers have made it their business to bring you a wide array of items that show the softer side of life, and they're open Friday through Monday. The Withers extend their hospitality at **The Little River Inn** (39307 John Mosby Highway), just a few doors down on the same side.

Owner Marcia Hall loves to shop, and the proof is in her store. **Diamonds and Rust** (39333 John Mosby Highway) is brimming with vintage beads, baubles, trinkets and retro fashions in a setting that's fun and fabulous.

Walk through the breezeway and into Bella Villa, a wonderland of shabby chic European and American antiques.

A mannequin sporting an early 20th century suit and cloak conjures up images of Sherlock Holmes, and a flapper dress and cloche will get you thinking about Halloween or even New Year's Eve. This is the place for affordable escapism.

Spangly purses, nostalgic charms, cameo necklaces and pocket watches fill the store, along with lacy linens and kitschy pictures. Diamonds and Rust is open daily but closed on Mondays.

The mother-daughter team of Kay Pitts and Margaret Hawes are ready to make you breakfast and more at their **Little Apple Pastry Shop** (23217 Meetinghouse Lane), an old fashioned country bakery with a case full of pies, cakes, cookies and treats.

A visit to Diamonds and Rust is a must, with its ever-changing inventory of retro fashions, jewelry and accessories.

Lauded by the *Washington Post* for light and flaky Southern Ham Biscuits and praised by the locals for their Everyday is Thanksgiving Turkey Sandwich, Kay and Margaret serve country comfort food with reckless abandon. Suffice it to say that diet is a four-letter word.

The Little Apple Pastry Shop is open Tuesday through Saturday and closes in mid-afternoon. Arrive by 10:30 a.m. if you'd like a breakfast sandwich, and note that the shop is closed on Sundays and Mondays.

Mary Ann and Tucker Withers welcome you to stay in their Little River Inn, a bed and breakfast in the heart of Aldie.

FYI:

- Make this trip on Saturdays from mid-April through mid-November.
- To learn more about the Aldie Mill, visit www.nvrpa.org.
- Visit individual websites for specific days and hours of operation.
- To learn about upcoming events, visit www.villageofaldie.com and www.aldieheritage.com.

Virginia's climate of warm days, cool nights and dependable rainfall produces
dozens of varieties to suit any taste.

Fall for Northern Virginia: Apples, apples, apples

It's not autumn without a visit to apple country, and this trip illustrates that, although pie is tasty, you can make more than pastry with fall's favorite fruit.

Our butts are smoking! That's the motto of the **Apple House** (4675 John Marshall Highway) in Linden, a homespun landmark that's proud of its BBQ. For over 50 years they've been giving happy wanderers a welcome stop on the way up to Skyline Drive or over to farm country.

The Apple House turns out breakfast, lunch and dinner from a tiny country kitchen, and at any time of day you can peek over the half-wall and see the spatulas flying. If you're not up for a meal, order the apple cider cinnamon donuts – made from a 1963 recipe – or the seasonal pumpkin donuts, available through the fall. Coffee is organic, freshly ground and delicious.

The gift shop features Christmas ornaments, an extensive array of Virginia products and an entire wall of hot sauce.

Stribling Orchard (11587 Poverty Hollow Lane) in Markham offers a day in the country, a bit of history and lots and lots of apples – about 2,500 trees worth – all within a one-hour drive from the city. On any given day a member of the sixth generation of farmers is on hand to show you around, answer questions and describe the many varieties of apples that are ripe for the picking.

Visit the check-in point to grab a map, a bag and a picker – that's not a personal shopper, it's a pole with a basket on top – and hit the hills. Stribling's trees are heavy with fruit, and the orchard is rich with the scent of the apples. A certain number find themselves under foot every season, sacrificing their lives to create an air freshener for the great outdoors.

A hike through 30 color-coded acres yields just the right picks for lunches and pies. Day trippers who make it to the top of the hill will be rewarded with breath-taking views of the Blue Ridge Mountains and Shenandoah Valley, much resembling a folk art painting. Several picnic tables offer a convenient place to linger.

Down at the **Harvest House** you can pay for your apples – by the pound, the peck or the bushel – and purchase apple pies, turnovers and breads, as well as the farm's preserves and honey.

This is the place to bump into a member of the Stribling clan and connect; the family loves to hear from the people who visit their orchard. One man has been coming to pick apples for over 50 years, and on a recent visit he brought a horde of great-grandchildren to pass the tradition on for another half-century or more.

A young family uses a picker to reach the ripe apples at treetop.

Chateau O'Brien sells apples for adults only.

Below the parking lot several historic buildings can be seen, although they are not open to the public. These include the 19th century smokehouse, dairy, summer kitchen and slave quarters.

A quick drive away – over the railroad tracks, to the right and over the tracks again – brings you to **Chateau O'Brien Winery** and their version of apples, for adults only. The O'Brien's Virginia Apple Wine is made from six varieties of Stribling's finest, with the blend tweaked every year to provide consistent taste and balance.

While this is deemed a dessert wine, it's not at all cloying; just think of biting into the best apple you ever tasted. Virginia Apple Wine pairs perfectly with a sharp cheese like cheddar or with a caramel-based dessert. It mulls well and also imparts layers of flavor to Thanksgiving turkeys and holiday hams.

Chateau O'Brien is especially known for its Cabernet Franc, Malbec, Petit Verdot, Tannat Limited Reserve and Late Harvest Tannat, and for several equally respectable white wines. Heat lamps on the patio and a fireplace off the tasting room make this a cozy spot as the weather cools, but it isn't a stop when you have the kids in tow. The winery doesn't allow anyone under the age of 21.

Detour up scenic Leeds Manor Road to Upperville for a bit of Ireland in Virginia Hunt County. **The Blackthorne Inn and Restaurant** (10087 John S. Mosby Highway) – formerly known at the 1763 Inn and currently owned by the O'Connor family – is in the tradition of a great wayside inn.

Whether you're in their dining room or in the Wolf Tone Pub, don't miss the Irish nachos. Blackstone's own freshly made potato chips are smothered with Dublin cheddar, sprinkled with applewood bacon and green onions and served with garlic cheese sauce. Dinner offerings lean toward gourmet fare, while pub food is informal and fun.

Stop by the Blackthorne Inn and Restaurant to experience a bit of Ireland.

The property was once owned by a young George Washington, and you may ask to see the deed. It's not known if our first president ever slept here, but you can – in one of the many comfortable cottages or cabins.

FYI:

- This trip should be made on a fall weekend before mid-October.
- For details about hours of operation, visit the individual websites.
- Pets are not allowed at Stribling Orchard, and children are not allowed at Chateau O'Brien.

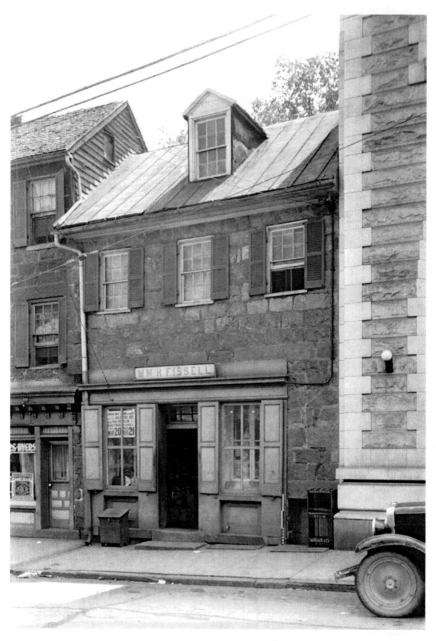

Main Street in Ellicott City appears much as it did in 1936, when captured in this photo by E. H. Pickering for the Historic American Building Survey.
Courtesy of the Library of Congress, Prints & Photographs Division

Festive Ellicott City: Everything old is new again

A visit to Ellicott City, Maryland lends an unmistakable feeling of déjà vu. Nostalgic buildings spanning three centuries feature purveyors of fine home furnishings, foods, gifts, antiques and collectibles – each with the picturesque storefronts and personalized service of a bygone era.

Soak in the ambiance with a stroll along around town, starting at the circa 1780 **Thomas Isaac Log Cabin** (8398 Main Street) on the west end. The oldest surviving residential structure in Howard County is now a Heritage Center that teaches the history of the region and recalls what life was like for the settlers of the Patapsco Valley.

The Historic District was designated in 1973 to preserve and encourage restoration of its structures, and you can take a walking tour using the free map that's available at the **Visitors Center** (8267 Main Street). This downtown has evolved quite nicely while retaining the look and feel of its humble roots.

This isn't Walt Disney's Main Street; it's yours and mine.

Ellicott City was the cradle of the Industrial Revolution in Maryland, founded as a tiny trade center for a flour mill established in 1772 by three Quaker brothers from Pennsylvania. The trio persuaded farmers to plant wheat instead of tobacco, and they built a thriving business on that agricultural twist of fate.

The town became home to the first terminus of the B&O Railroad outside Baltimore in 1830, and the **B&O Ellicott City Railroad Station** (2711 Maryland Avenue) is designated the oldest surviving station in America. Located on the east end of town, it's now a museum that offers something for every member of the family.

A landmark B&O railroad bridge greets visitors, adding to Ellicott City's 19th century flavor.

Exhibits are set up in rooms labeled by purpose – Men's Waiting Room, Women's Waiting Room, Telegraph Office – revealing how the station functioned in its heyday. Sitting on a bench in one of the rooms, you can almost feel the thunder of a steam locomotive coming down the tracks.

In addition to the Freight House's permanent HO layout, the annual Holiday Festival offers a Thomas the Tank operating G-scale layout, an O-scale crazy train layout, a push button children's layout, and a brand new multi-level, O-scale model train layout that took over 750 hours for three full-time builders to complete. The holiday displays are featured in December and January each year.

In Ellicott City, everything old is new again – a Post Office turned Visitors Center, a row house reinvented as an antique emporium and an old-fashioned movie theater featuring Boyd Bears on the marquee.

Antiques reign supreme, in addition to stores selling everything from upscale apparel for dogs at the **Yuppy Puppy Pet Boutique** (8120 Main Street) to sea glass earrings for his best friend at **Art and Artisan** (8020 Main Street). **Mumbles and Squeaks Toy Shoppe** (8133 Main Street) has been touted by the *Washington Post a*s a child's fantasy brought to life, and **Sweet Cascades** (8167 Main Street) has earned the distinction of a Best of Baltimore award for its unusual ingredients and innovative packaging.

Ah, Sweet Cascades. This delightfully decadent candy store is packed with both old fashioned favorites and newfangled flavors. Owners Sue and Rick Whary have a way with chocolate – enthusiastically enrobing just about anything that doesn't walk with the food of the gods – and the results are never boring. You can buy a bag of goodies and decide for yourself what works and what doesn't.

Popular items include the chocolate-covered pork rinds, bacon, Doritos, beefy jerky, jalapeno peppers and Cheetos, all making the chocolate-coated Fluffer Nutters look almost pedestrian. The shop is best known for its Old-Bay-flavored chocolates crabs, an unexpectedly pleasant compliment to beer. Maryland made and microbrewed, of course.

The Freight Agent's living quarters are recreated to appear as if he just stepped out for a coffee break.

The award-winning **Ellicott Mills Brewing Company** (8308 Main Street) boasts eight beers on tap, with four-glass flights priced under $10. Growler refills are also available with a deposit. An extensive menu offers soups, salads, burgers, steaks, lobsters and, for the more adventurous diner, wild game.

The owners of Sweet Cascades will share their philosophy on enrobing snack foods with chocolate if given the opportunity.

At the **Judge's Bench Pub** (8385 Main Street) you can have your history and eat it, too – the premier tap house was actually Howard County's courthouse in the 1800s. While taverns remain a popular favorite, other cuisines are also represented with restaurants serving everything from traditional British afternoon tea to Japanese-American fusion.

Other points of historic interest include the **Firehouse Museum** (3829 Church Road) – the county's first fire station – now showcasing firefighting memorabilia and equipment, and the ruins of the **Patapsco Female Institute** (3655 Church Road), structurally stabilized to become the centerpiece of a historic park. Hours at the attractions are limited in the winter, so it's best to focus on the numerous shops and restaurants if you visit in the colder months.

The old-fashioned, unadulterated five-and-dime-store flavor of Ellicott City may remind you of somewhere you've been before. If you're from the Northeast that might be a mill town like Lowell, Massachusetts, and if you're native to the West it could be one of the silver and gold rush magnets, like Leadville, Colorado.

Ellicott City is our very own slice of small town Americana, right in Washington, DC's backyard. A visit recalls an era when we didn't shop online or at the mall. Once upon a time we knew the shopkeepers by name and could chat with them about their wares, asking important questions like, "Why bacon?"

FYI:

- The B&O Railroad Museum is open daily but closed on holidays.
- For additional information, visit www.borail.org.
- Admission fee varies by age.
- Parking is abundant and free at several municipal lots.

Carpe Weekend's tip:

Purchase a combo ticket for an additional $2 and visit the B&O Museum or the Mount Clare Museum House in Baltimore, too. Add $4 to your ticket and visit all three museums. The discounted combination ticket is valid for six months from the date of purchase.

Jamey Turner finds the uncommon in the common, making beautiful music
with wine glasses and water.

Year Round Alexandria: Have a blast

The Torpedo Factory Arts Center is a thriving year round celebration of the arts, situated on the scenic waterfront in Old Town Alexandria, Virginia. Here more than 160 artists work in studios spread over three floors, connected by an extensive system of catwalks.

I'm pickin' up good vibrations ... And they're coming from the corner, just outside the front door of the **Torpedo Factory** (105 N. Union Street). Here inspiration travels through the air, along with music from a most unlikely source – brandy snifters.

On most weekends **Jamey Turner** sets up his glass harp and plays everything from Beethoven to Brubeck. I recently had the pleasure of standing on the fringe of his makeshift stage, closing my eyes for a moment and savoring music Thomas Jefferson might have enjoyed – Yankee Doodle Dandy and The Star Spangled Banner – produced on an instrument he admired. But unlike Jefferson, I had the added benefit of anecdotes from a quirky street musician.

Turner has appeared at the Kennedy Center, in *National Geographic Magazine* and on *The Tonight Show* for his rare talent – he's one of only a few dozen people in the world who has mastered an instrument that was invented in 1741 and made popular throughout the remainder of the 18th century.

Prepare to be amazed as he works dozens of snifters that are partially filled with water – distilled, never tap – to produce the perfect pitch. He tells his audience about molecular integrity and the intonation that's gained from H_2O that's free of minerals and chemicals. But the bottom line is that this man makes barware sing.

Inside the Torpedo Factory, many of the artists are on site creating watercolors, prints, textiles, jewelry, glassware and photographic arts. It's fun to walk through the maze of color and creativity, chatting with them about their labors of love. And there's no better way for kids to learn an appreciation for art than to meet the people who create it.

The history of the place is inspirational, too, providing the perfect example of how a center for the arts can revitalize a community. The Torpedo Factory began life as a factory for the manufacture of torpedo shell casings in 1918 and operated through WWII. In 1969 the city of Alexandria purchased the building, and in 1974 it opened to the public. The development of the waterfront area followed, and soon the good times rolled.

Today the Torpedo Factory plays host to over 500,000 visitors per year and serves as a model for visual arts centers around the world. Featured artists must pass a jury review before they are considered for studio space. And the work you see has all been created right here.

Observe artists and purchase their original works at a weapons factory turned art center.

Artists are often found happily creating art in their studios at the Torpedo Factory.

On the third floor is the **Alexandria Archeological Museum and Research Lab**, where Alexandria digs its past. A current exhibit uses the excavation of a city block to reveal the steps of the archeological process and the history of Alexandria, with representations of 18th century wharves and early 19th century homes, shops, taverns and warehouses.

Volunteers can be found in the archaeology lab on most Fridays, washing, marking or cataloguing items from a recent site or working with artifacts.

The Torpedo Factory offers numerous events throughout the year, and most are free to the public. The Spring Open House is featured on Mothers' Day every year and filled with artist demonstrations, live music, hands-on activities and refreshments in the form of sparkling wine and treats.

Good feelings spill right out the back door and onto the boardwalk, where recreational craft is docked, food and beverages are sold, street music is enjoyed, and the Potomac Riverboat Company shoves off for tours of the harbor.

Old Town is home to dozens of interesting shops and award winning restaurants, several of which are owned by the EatGoodFood Group, and in 2012 the fabulous foodies launched **Society Fair** (277 S. Washington Street). This is not your average emporium of good things to eat; it's a place of worship, too.

Cozy up to the stylish wine bar and order a mid-day snack or light lunch, accompanied by a glass of fine wine. Oh, so civilized.

Your server will be happy to recommend just the right wine to pair with eclectic sandwiches, such as My Turkish Cousin (lamb shoulder, preserved lemon yogurt, sultana mostarda and sautéed spinach on flatbread). From this vantage point you can watch signature drinks being made, food being savored and people having fun.

Attention to detail and a fun approach make Society Fair a foodie haven.

You may not want to leave your perch, but when you do be sure to check out the goodies in the bakery, butchery and cheese shop. This is the place to forage for the ingredients to make a kickass antipasto. Or take home a slice of from-scratch coconut or carrot cake, and you'll never buy the stuff at the grocery store again. Society Fair is a much-needed celebration that presents food as art, with a touch of whimsy.

FYI:

- The Torpedo Factory is open daily except on major holidays.
- Admission is free and well-mannered, leashed dogs are welcome.
- Visit www.torpedofactory.org for additional information.
- Garage parking is found on N. Union Street.
- A free trolley operates between the waterfront and the Metro.
- Society Fair is open Monday through Sunday.
- Check their website at www.societyfair.net for hours.
- Metered, on-street parking is accessible.

Carpe Weekend's tip:

The Torpedo Factory is open until 9 p.m. on Thursdays and hosts free activities on the second Thursday night of each month. Art lovers visit open studios and galleries, chat with the artists and enjoy receptions and refreshments throughout the year. Themes vary with the seasons, and the November celebration – *FotoWeekDC* – is especially popular.

ABOUT US

Elaine and Paul Jean are empty nesters with an incurable case of wanderlust. Elaine is a nonfiction writer and has contributed hundreds of columns and feature stories to local newspapers, including the *Loudoun Independent*, the *Loudoun Times-Mirror* and the *Fairfax County Times*.

Paul is a mild-mannered engineering manager by day and a freelance photographer to his core. Over three decades ago the couple became husband and wife, and in 2010 they married Elaine's words to Paul's photos while exploring the Mid-Atlantic region. Together they founded the website *www.roamingtheplanet.com* in 2011.

Elaine and Paul have become addicted to day tripping, and now they're inviting you to come along.

Carpe Weekend!

A Roamingtheplanet.com Guide

Single Step Press
Potomac Falls, Virginia

CPSIA information can be obtained at www.ICGtesting.com
Printed in the USA
LVOW06s1552120314

377119LV00008BA/172/P